101 Things®
To Do With
Beer

101 Things To Do With Beer

BY ELIZA CROSS

GIBBS SMITH
TO ENRICH AND INSPIRE HUMANKIND

First Edition
20 19 18 17 16   5 4 3 2 1

Published by
Gibbs Smith
P.O. Box 667
Layton, Utah 84041

1.800.835.4993 orders
www.gibbs-smith.com

Printed and bound in Korea
Gibbs Smith books are printed on either recycled, 100% post-consumer
waste, FSC-certified papers or on paper produced from sustainable PEFC-
certified forest/controlled wood source. Learn more at www.pefc.org.

Library of Congress Cataloging-in-Publication Data

Names: Cross, Eliza, author.
Title: 101 things to do with beer / Eliza Cross.
Other titles: One hundred one things to do with beer
 | One hundred and one things to do with beer
Description: First edition. | Layton, Utah : Gibbs
Smith, [2016] | Includes index.
Identifiers: LCCN 2016000321 | ISBN 9781423643029 (pbk.)
Subjects: LCSH: Cooking (Beer) | LCGFT: Cookbooks.
Classification: LCC TX726.3 .C76 2016 | DDC 641.6/23--dc23
LC record available at http://lccn.loc.gov/2016000321
ISBN 13: 978-1-4236-4302-9

For C.J. Holloway, always effervescent.

www.gibbs-smith.com

CONTENTS

Helpful Hints 9

Dinners

One-Pan Beer Onion Chicken 68 • Beer Bacon Mac and Cheese 69 • Beer-Inated Grilled Pork Chops 70 • Beer Cheese Fondue 71 • Beer-Simmered Sausage and Rice 72 • Beer Barbecue Slow Cooker Ribs 73 • Beer Boiled Shrimp 74 • Beef and Stout Potpie 75 • Chicken and Dumplings 76 • Welsh Rarebit 77 • Beer-Simmered Chicken Tacos 78 • Crispy Beer Batter Fish Filets 79 • Extra Crispy Fried Chicken 80 • Beer Can Chicken 81 • Slow Cooker Beer French Dip 82 • Easy Glazed Corned Beef 83 • Grilled Beer Bratwurst 84 • Best Beef Brisket 85 • Spaghetti with Beer-Braised Meatballs 86 • Spicy Sweet Slow-Cooked Pulled Pork 87 • Chicken and Mushroom Risotto 88 • Honey Mustard Roast Pork 89 • Italian Beef 90 • Beer-Braised Pot Roast 91 • Beer and Molasses Glazed BBQ Chicken 92

Side Dishes

Bacon, Cheddar, and Beer Potatoes Au Gratin 94 • Buttered Mushrooms with Thyme 95 • German Potato Salad with Beer Dressing 96 • Creamy Cheddar and Beer Broccoli 97 • Beans, Bacon, and Beer 98 • Grilled Corn with Chile Lime Butter 99 • German Green Beans 100 • Beer-Braised Garlic Parmesan Acorn Squash 101 • Cheesy Beer Hash Browns 102 • Beer Refrigerator Pickles 103 • Beer-Glazed Carrots 104 • Sweet and Sour Pale Ale Coleslaw 105

Desserts

Chocolate Stout Cake with Cream Cheese Frosting 108 • Apple Cinnamon Beer Batter Crepes 109 • Cherry Beery Bundt Cake 110 • Spicy Gingerbread Cake 111 • Chocolate Glazed Stout Brownies 112 • Chocolate Stout Ice Cream 113 • Irish Cheesecake 114 • Vanilla Beer Cake 115 • Beer-Battered Caramel Bananas 116

Sweets

Stout Almond Brittle 118 • Beer Pretzel Truffles 119 • Chocolate Stout Fudge 120 • Beer Caramel Corn 121 • Beer Sea Salt Caramels 122 • Beer-Glazed Peanuts 123

HELPFUL HINTS

1. Each type of beer has a distinctive flavor profile that can enhance foods. These are the basic types of beer:

Pilsner is a crisp lager with a lightly bitter flavor.

Bock beer is a strong, darker lager with malty flavors.

Wheat beer is often unfiltered, with a mellow, fruity flavor.

Pale ale is crisp, with a bitter, hoppy flavor.

IPA and **Double IPA** are bitter with more aggressive hops and malt flavors.

Porter is a dark, medium-bodied beer with malty sweet and bitter hops flavors.

Stout is a dark, heavy beer with toasty coffee and chocolate flavors.

2. Non-alcoholic, low-alcohol (3.2%), and light (low-calorie) beers can be substituted for regular beer in many recipes, but the beer flavor may be less pronounced.

3. Do not use non-alcoholic beers in baking recipes, since the yeast in regular beer acts as a leavening agent.

4. Beer makes an excellent marinade for meats, as its enzymes have a tenderizing effect. When grilling beer-marinated meats, the beer's natural sugars help promote browning and caramelizing.

5. Since beer doesn't have as much acidity as wine, meats can be marinated for a longer period of time (up to 48 hours) and absorb more flavor.

6. When adding beer to a mixture, use a larger mixing bowl since beer can foam up upon contact with other ingredients.

7. Once beer is added to a batter, handle it gently. Stirring too vigorously can reduce the bubbles and lessen the beer's leavening qualities.

8. Baked goods made with beer generally have a longer shelf life and moister texture than those made without beer.

9. When cooking with very bitter beers, adding a touch of brown sugar, maple syrup, or honey may help balance the flavors.

10. When cooking with alcoholic beer, some alcohol may remain in the dish. In general, the longer a dish is cooked, the less alcohol remains.

11. Because even small amounts of alcohol can be a problem for some people, advise guests if a dish has been prepared with beer.

12. Use caution when cooking with beer in foods that will be frozen, as the alcohol can inhibit the freezing process.

APPETIZERS

EASY BEER CHEESE DIP

1 package (8 ounces)	**cream cheese,** softened
1 cup	**sour cream**
$^1/_3$ cup	**regular or non-alcoholic beer**
1 envelope	**ranch salad dressing mix**
2 cups (8 ounces)	**grated cheddar cheese**
	pretzels or pita chips

In a large bowl, beat the cream cheese, sour cream, beer, and dressing mix until smooth. Stir in cheddar cheese. Serve with pretzels or pita chips. Makes about 3 $^1/_2$ cups.

BEER-BATTERED CAULIFLOWER

1 cup	**flour**
1 1/2 teaspoons	**baking powder**
1/2 teaspoon	**salt**
1/4 teaspoon	**garlic powder**
1/4 teaspoon	**onion powder**
1/4 teaspoon	**pepper**
2 tablespoons	**grated Parmesan cheese**
1 cup	**lager beer**
4 cups	**fresh cauliflower florets**
	peanut oil, for frying
2/3 cup	**ranch dressing**

In a large bowl, whisk together the flour, baking powder, salt, garlic powder, onion powder, pepper, cheese, and beer until smooth. Add cauliflower florets and toss until well coated with batter.

In deep fryer or heavy saucepan, heat about 3 inches of oil to 375 degrees. Fry cauliflower in batches, turning once, until golden brown, about 2–3 minutes. Drain on paper towels.

Serve warm with ranch dressing for dipping. Makes 8 servings.

GOLDEN BEER CHEESE PUFFS

I cup	**beer**
$1/4$ cup	**butter**
I cup	**flour**
I teaspoon	**Worcestershire sauce**
$1/2$ teaspoon	**salt**
$1/8$ teaspoon	**cayenne pepper**
I $1/2$ cups	**grated Swiss cheese**
4	**eggs**

Preheat oven to 400 degrees. Prepare a baking sheet with nonstick cooking spray.

Combine beer and butter in a medium saucepan. Bring to a boil. Add flour all at once and beat until mixture forms a ball. Remove from heat. Add Worcestershire sauce, salt, cayenne pepper, and cheese. Beat until cheese melts and mixture is blended and smooth. Add eggs, one at a time beating well after each addition.

Drop by teaspoonfuls on prepared baking sheet. Bake until golden brown, about 20 minutes. Cool on wire rack. Makes 8 servings.

CRISPY BEER CHICKEN WINGS

1 tablespoon	**packed brown sugar**
1 tablespoon	**salt**
1 can or bottle (12 ounces)	**beer**
2 pounds	**chicken wings**
$^1/_4$ cup	**butter**
$^1/_4$ cup	**hot pepper sauce**
2 teaspoons	**cornstarch**
1 $^1/_2$ teaspoons	**garlic powder**
1 $^1/_2$ teaspoons	**onion powder**
1 $^1/_2$ teaspoons	**paprika**
$^1/_4$ teaspoon	**cayenne pepper**
$^2/_3$ cup	**blue cheese dressing**

Preheat oven to 350 degrees. Line a baking sheet with aluminum foil and spray lightly with nonstick cooking spray.

In a large bowl, combine the brown sugar, salt, and beer; whisk to combine. Add chicken wings and toss gently to coat. Cover and refrigerate for 1 hour. In a 1-quart saucepan, melt butter. In a small bowl, whisk together the hot pepper sauce and cornstarch. Add to the butter and whisk to combine. Heat to a simmer, remove from heat and reserve.

In a large ziplock bag, combine the garlic powder, onion powder, paprika, and cayenne pepper. Remove wings from beer mixture, pat dry with paper towels, and discard beer mixture. Add wings to bag with seasonings and shake until evenly coated. Arrange on prepared baking sheet and pour hot sauce mixture over wings. Bake for 30–35 minutes, or until an instant read thermometer registers 165 degrees on thickest part of chicken. Serve with blue cheese dressing. Makes 6 servings.

BEER CANDIED BACON

1/3 cup	**regular or non-alcoholic beer**
1/4 cup	**packed dark brown sugar**
1/4 cup	**maple syrup**
1 pound	**thick-sliced bacon**
2 teaspoons	**pepper**

Preheat oven to 400 degrees. Line a rimmed baking sheet with aluminum foil.

Combine beer, brown sugar, and maple syrup in a small bowl, whisking well to dissolve sugar. Reserve.

Arrange the bacon on prepared baking sheet, overlapping if necessary. Place in oven and cook for 10 minutes. Reduce temperature to 275 degrees, remove pan from oven, and blot the rendered fat from the bacon with a paper towel.

Brush both sides of each strip of bacon with the beer syrup. Return to oven and cook for 10 minutes. Remove from oven and brush both sides with syrup. Turn bacon over and cook for 10 minutes. Remove from oven, brush both sides with syrup and sprinkle with pepper. Turn bacon over and cook until crispy and browned, about 8 minutes. Cool for 10 minutes before serving. Makes 6 servings.

GARLIC PARMESAN ONION RINGS

1 cup plus 1 tablespoon	**flour,** divided
$1/4$ teaspoon	**salt,** plus extra for sprinkling
$1/4$ teaspoon	**garlic powder**
$1/8$ teaspoon	**cayenne pepper**
1 cup	**lager beer**
1	**large sweet onion,** such as Vidalia, cut in $1/3$-inch slices
	peanut oil, for frying
2 tablespoons	**grated Parmesan cheese**

In a medium bowl, whisk together 1 cup flour, $1/4$ teaspoon salt, garlic powder, and cayenne pepper. Make a well in the center, pour in the beer and whisk just until smooth. Cover with plastic wrap and let rest at room temperature for 1 hour.

Put the remaining 1 tablespoon flour in a large ziplock bag. Separate the onion slices, place in the bag and shake until evenly coated with flour. In deep fryer or heavy saucepan, heat about 3 inches of oil to 375 degrees.

Working in batches, dip the onion rings in the beer batter to coat and fry in the hot oil, turning once, until golden brown, about 2–3 minutes. Transfer to paper towels to drain, and sprinkle with salt and Parmesan cheese. Makes 6 servings.

LIGHT AND CRISPY
ONION SHOESTRINGS

$1/2$ cup	**flour**
$1/2$ cup	**lager beer**
1	**egg,** lightly beaten
1 teaspoon	**seasoned salt**
$1/2$ teaspoon	**baking powder**
1	**large onion,** halved lengthwise and cut in $1/8$-inch slices
	peanut oil, for frying
	salt

In a shallow bowl, whisk together the flour, beer, egg, seasoned salt, and baking powder.

In a deep fryer or heavy saucepan, heat 3 inches of oil to 375 degrees. Separate onion slices. Working in batches, dip the onion slices in the beer batter to coat and shake off excess. Fry, turning once, until golden brown, about 1−2 minutes. Transfer to paper towels to drain, sprinkle with salt, and serve immediately. Makes 6 servings.

BEER BARBECUE KIELBASA BITES

1 1/2 cups	**regular or non-alcoholic beer**
1 1/2 cups	**barbecue sauce**
1/2 cup	**brown sugar**
1/4 cup	**Dijon mustard**
2 pounds	**kielbasa sausage,** cut in 1/2-inch slices

Combine the beer, barbecue sauce, brown sugar, and mustard in a large frying pan over medium heat. Bring to a boil, stirring occasionally; reduce heat to low and add the kielbasa. Simmer stirring occasionally until kielbasa is browned and glazed, about 1 hour. Use a slotted spoon to transfer to a platter and serve with toothpicks. Makes 12 servings.

ALE CARAMELIZED ONION AND BACON DIP

2	**large onions**
2 tablespoons	**olive oil**
$^3/_4$ cup	**amber ale**
2 cloves	**garlic,** peeled and minced
8 ounces	**cream cheese,** softened
1 cup	**sour cream**
4 slices	**thick-cut bacon,** cooked, drained, and crumbled
	salt and pepper, to taste
2	**green onions,** chopped
	pita or bagel chips

Quarter the onions, and cut each quarter in $^1/_4$-inch slices. Heat the olive oil in a large frying pan over medium heat. Add the onions and cook, stirring frequently, until transparent, about 6 minutes. Lower the heat to medium-low, cover and cook, stirring occasionally, until onions are light brown and starting to caramelize, about 25–30 minutes.

Remove the lid and add the ale. Increase heat to medium and cook, stirring frequently, until most of the liquid cooks away and onions are deep golden brown. Add the garlic and cook for 1 minute. Remove from heat.

In a medium bowl combine the cream cheese and sour cream; stir until well blended. Add the caramelized onions and bacon and stir until well combined. Season with salt and pepper and garnish with chopped green onions. Serve with pita or bagel chips. Makes 8 servings.

BACON-WRAPPED BEER BRATS

4	**bratwurst sausages**
I can or bottle (12 ounces)	**regular or non-alcoholic beer**
6 tablespoons	**brown sugar**
$^1/_2$ teaspoon	**pepper**
$^1/_4$ teaspoon	**cayenne pepper**
8 slices	**bacon,** cut in half

Poke bratwurst sausages several times with a small fork, and arrange in a medium frying pan over high heat. Pour the beer around the bratwurst and bring to a boil. Reduce heat to low, cover and simmer for 15 minutes. Remove the bratwurst from the beer, and drain on paper towels. Discard the beer.

Preheat oven to 425 degrees. Line a baking sheet with aluminum foil, place a wire rack on top, and set aside.

In a medium bowl, combine the brown sugar, pepper, and cayenne pepper; reserve.

Cut each bratwurst in 4 pieces, wrap each piece with half strip of bacon, and secure with a toothpick. Toss the bratwurst in the brown sugar mixture to coat, and arrange on the wire rack on the prepared baking sheet. Bake, turning once, until the bacon is brown and crisp, 25–35 minutes. Makes 8 servings.

BEER-BATTERED JALAPENO CHIPS

1 cup	**flour**
1 teaspoon	**salt**
1/2 teaspoon	**chili powder**
1/2 teaspoon	**cumin**
1/4 teaspoon	**garlic powder**
1/4 teaspoon	**pepper**
1 cup	**lager beer**
	peanut oil, for frying
12	**large jalapenos,** seeds removed, cut in 1/3-inch slices
	salt
1 cup	**ranch dressing**

In a medium bowl, whisk together the flour, salt, chili powder, cumin, garlic powder, and pepper. Add the beer and whisk just until smooth. Cover with plastic wrap and rest at room temperature for 1 hour.

In a deep fryer or heavy saucepan, heat 2 inches of oil to 375 degrees. Working in batches, dip the jalapeno slices in the beer batter to coat and fry, turning once, until golden brown, about 2–3 minutes. Transfer to paper towels to drain, and sprinkle with salt. Serve with ranch dressing. Makes 8 servings.

CERVEZA CON QUESO DIP

2 cups	**grated sharp cheddar cheese**
2 cups	**grated Monterey Jack cheese**
2 tablespoons	**flour**
I tablespoon	**butter**
I	**small onion,** minced
I	**jalapeno pepper,** seeds removed, diced
$^3/_4$ cup	**light beer**
I	**tomato,** seeds and pulp removed, diced
	scoop-style corn chips

Combine the cheddar and Monterey Jack cheeses in a large bowl.
Sprinkle with the flour and toss with a fork to coat cheese; reserve.

In a large, heavy saucepan, melt the butter over medium heat and
cook the onion and jalapeno, stirring frequently, until softened, about
5 minutes. Add the beer and tomato, and simmer the mixture for 5
minutes. Add reserved cheese $^1/_2$ cup at a time to the beer mixture,
stirring after each addition until the cheeses are melted, and well
incorporated. Serve with chips. Makes $4^1/_2$ cups.

BEER CHEESE CRACKERS

8 ounces	**extra sharp cheddar cheese,** grated
4 tablespoons	**cold butter,** cut in cubes
$^1/_2$ teaspoon	**salt**
1 cup	**flour,** plus extra for sprinkling
4 tablespoons	**cold beer**

In the bowl of a food processor, mix together cheese, butter, and salt until well combined. Add the flour and pulse just until pea-sized pieces form. Slowly add 1 tablespoon of beer at a time with motor running, just until the dough begins to form into a ball. (You may not need all of the beer.) Gather dough together and form a $^1/_2$-inch thick disk. Wrap with plastic wrap and refrigerate for 1−2 hours, or overnight.

Preheat oven to 350 degrees. Line a baking sheet with parchment paper.

On a lightly floured surface, roll dough into a rectangle, $^1/_8$ inch thick. Cut dough into 1-inch squares using a fluted pastry wheel or pizza cutter. Poke a hole in the center of each cracker with a toothpick or skewer. Transfer to prepared baking sheet, leaving $^1/_2$ inch of space around each cracker. Bake for 15−20 minutes, until puffed and beginning to brown around the edges. Transfer crackers to a wire rack to cool. Store in an airtight container for up to 5 days. Makes about 80 crackers.

mini corn dogs

¹/4 cup	**cornstarch**
12 (12-inch)	**bamboo skewers,** each cut in half
8	**hot dogs,** each cut in 3 equal pieces
1 ¹/4 cups	**flour**
³/4 cup	**cornmeal**
3 tablespoons	**sugar**
1 teaspoon	**baking powder**
1 teaspoon	**salt**
2	**eggs**
³/4 cup	**lager beer**
	peanut oil, for frying
	ketchup and mustard

Pour the cornstarch in a small bowl. Thread the end of each skewer with 1 hot dog piece. Dredge the hot dogs in cornstarch, gently tapping off excess.

In a large bowl, whisk together the flour, cornmeal, sugar, baking powder, and salt. In a small bowl, whisk together eggs and beer and stir into flour mixture until well combined and smooth; reserve.

Fill a deep-fryer or Dutch oven with 2 inches of oil, and heat to 375 degrees.

Pour the batter in a tall glass, which will make it easier to dip the hot dogs evenly. Holding the ends of the skewers, dip the hot dogs into the batter until completely covered. Carefully fry the battered hot dogs, on the skewers, in the hot oil in batches until golden brown, 2–3 minutes. Drain on paper towels. Serve with ketchup and mustard. Makes 24 pieces.

STOUT-GLAZED CHICKEN SKEWERS

1/2 cup	**stout beer,** such as Guinness
1/3 cup	**honey**
1/4 cup	**soy sauce**
2 cloves	**garlic,** peeled and minced
1 teaspoon	**red pepper flakes**
1/2 teaspoon	**Dijon mustard**
1/4 teaspoon	**pepper**
6	**boneless, skinless chicken thigh fillets,** cut in 1-inch pieces
12 (6-inch)	**wooden or bamboo skewers**
1 tablespoon	**olive oil**
1	**medium shallot,** peeled and minced
	vegetable oil
	minced green onion

In a small bowl, whisk together the beer, honey, soy sauce, garlic, red pepper flakes, mustard, and pepper. Add the chicken, toss to coat, and cover and refrigerate for 1–2 hours. Soak the skewers in warm water for 30 minutes; drain on paper towels. Remove chicken from beer mixture (do not discard), and thread chicken through the skewers. Place on a plate and set aside.

In a small saucepan over medium-high heat, add the olive oil and shallots. Cook, stirring frequently, until softened, about 5 minutes. Add remaining beer mixture and boil, stirring frequently, until reduced and thickened, about 8 minutes. Remove from heat and reserve. Preheat grill to medium-high and brush grate with oil. Brush the chicken skewers with the glaze and arrange on the grill. Brush with glaze and turn every 2 minutes until cooked through, about 10 minutes. Garnish with minced green onion to serve. Makes 12 skewers.

BREADS

EASY SWISS CHEESY BEER BREAD

3 cups	**flour**
3 tablespoons	**sugar**
3 teaspoons	**baking powder**
1 $1/2$ teaspoons	**salt**
$1/2$ teaspoon	**pepper**
1 can or bottle (12 ounces)	**lager beer**
2 ounces	**Swiss cheese,** grated
2 ounces	**Swiss cheese,** cut in $1/4$-inch cubes
2 tablespoons	**butter,** melted

Preheat oven to 375 degrees. Prepare a 4 x 8-inch loaf pan with nonstick cooking spray.

In a large bowl, whisk together the flour, sugar, baking powder, salt, and pepper. Slowly add the beer and stir just until moistened. Fold in the cheeses.

Spread the batter in the prepared pan and drizzle with the melted butter. Bake until a toothpick inserted into the center comes out clean, 50–60 minutes. Cool for 10 minutes before removing from pan to a wire rack. Makes 1 loaf.

BEER-BATTERED APPLE FRITTERS

2	**large tart, crisp apples,** such as Granny Smith, peeled, cored, and chopped
1/4 cup	**packed light brown sugar**
2 tablespoons	**sugar**
1/2 teaspoon	**cinnamon**
1/8 teaspoon	**nutmeg**
1 cup	**flour**
1/4 teaspoon	**salt**
1 cup	**lager beer,** divided
	peanut oil, for frying
	powdered sugar

In a medium bowl, combine the apples, brown sugar, sugar, cinnamon, and nutmeg; stir.

In a large bowl, whisk together the flour and salt. Make a well in the center of the flour mixture and whisk in 7/8 cup of beer until combined. Mixture should be slightly thicker than pancake batter; add more beer if needed. Gently fold in the apple mixture and rest for 10 minutes.

In a deep fryer or Dutch oven, heat 3 inches of oil to 360 degrees. Working in batches, carefully drop the dough by rounded tablespoonfuls into the hot oil. Fry until golden brown on both sides, flipping once, about 4 minutes total. Drain on paper towels and sprinkle with powdered sugar. Makes 6 servings.

LIGHT-AS-A-FEATHER DOUGHNUT HOLES

2^1/2 cups	**flour**
^{1}/4 cup	**sugar**
I packet (2^1/4 teaspoons)	**rapid rise yeast**
^{1}/4 teaspoon	**nutmeg**
^{3}/4 cup	**lager beer**
3	**egg yolks,** room temperature
^{1}/4 cup	**heavy cream,** room temperature
I teaspoon	**salt**
^{1}/2 teaspoon	**vanilla**
	peanut oil, for frying
	powdered sugar

Line a baking sheet with parchment paper. In the bowl of a stand mixer fitted with a dough hook, combine the flour, sugar, yeast, and nutmeg. Add the beer to a microwave-safe bowl and heat in 10 second increments until thermometer measures 125 degrees. Add the beer to the flour mixture and beat on medium-high until combined. Continue beating, adding the egg yolks, one at a time. Add the cream, salt, and vanilla. Transfer dough to a lightly oiled bowl, cover and let rise at room temperature until doubled in size, about I hour. Punch down dough, knead lightly to remove any air bubbles, return to bowl, cover and refrigerate for I hour. Roll dough on a lightly floured surface to I-inch thickness and cut with a 2-inch round cutter, rerolling scraps. Place doughnut holes on prepared baking sheet and cover loosely with a towel. Let rise at room temperature until doubled in size, about 30 minutes.

In a large saucepan, heat I inch of oil to 350 degrees. Working in batches, fry the doughnuts on each side about 1–2 minutes until golden brown. Remove from oil, drain on paper towels, and cool on a wire rack. Sprinkle with powdered sugar and serve. Makes about 24 doughnut holes.

EASY BEER BISCUITS

4 cups	**biscuit mix**
$^1/_4$ cup	**sugar**
1 can or bottle (12 ounces)	**lager beer**
2 tablespoons	**butter,** melted
	milk or cream, for brushing

Preheat oven to 400 degrees. Lightly prepare an 8 x 8-inch baking dish with nonstick cooking spray; set aside.

In a large bowl, combine the biscuit mix, sugar, beer, and melted butter and stir just until mixture comes together. Turn out onto a floured surface and knead 3–4 times, just enough to make a soft dough.

Roll dough to a thickness of $^1/_2$ inch. Cut biscuits with a 2-inch round cutter and arrange in the prepared baking dish, brushing the tops with milk or cream. Bake for about 15–20 minutes, or until bottoms are golden brown. Makes 16 biscuits

BEER, BACON, AND CHEDDAR CORNBREAD

1 1/2 cups	**cornmeal**
1 1/2 cups	**flour**
2 tablespoons	**sugar**
1 1/2 tablespoons	**baking powder**
3/4 teaspoon	**salt**
1 1/2 cups	**grated sharp cheddar cheese,** divided
3	**eggs**
1/2 cup	**milk**
1/3 cup	**sour cream**
1 cup	**lager beer**
1/2 cup	**butter,** melted
6 slices	**thick-cut bacon,** fried and crumbled

Preheat oven to 375 degrees. Lightly prepare a 9 x 13-inch baking dish with nonstick cooking spray.

In a large bowl, combine the cornmeal, flour, sugar, baking powder, salt, and 1/2 cup of cheese.

In a medium bowl, combine the eggs, milk, sour cream, beer, and melted butter; stir until well blended. Add the liquid mixture to the cornmeal mixture and stir until just combined. Add the bacon and stir to incorporate throughout the batter. Spread in the prepared baking dish and sprinkle the remaining 1 cup of cheese over the top. Bake until lightly browned and a toothpick inserted into the center comes out clean, about 30–35 minutes. Cut in squares. Makes 12 servings.

CARAWAY BEER BREAD

3 cups	**flour**
I tablespoon	**baking powder**
I tablespoon	**sugar**
I teaspoon	**salt**
I can or bottle (I2 ounces)	**lager beer,** room temperature
2 tablespoons	**caraway seeds**
2 tablespoons	**butter,** melted

Preheat oven to 350 degrees. Lightly prepare a 9 x 5-inch loaf pan with nonstick cooking spray.

In a large bowl, whisk together the flour, baking powder, sugar, and salt. Make a well in the center. Add beer and caraway seeds to well; stir just until blended. Spread in prepared pan.

Bake for 50 minutes. Remove from the oven and brush top with half the melted butter. Bake I0 more minutes, or until lightly browned. Remove loaf to a cooling rack and brush the top with the remaining butter. Cool for I5 minutes before slicing. Makes I loaf.

SOFT BEER PRETZELS

1 bottle (12 ounces)	**amber ale**
1 package (¹/₄ ounce)	**active dry yeast**
2 tablespoons	**butter,** melted
2 tablespoons	**sugar**
1¹/₂ teaspoons	**salt**
4–4¹/₂ cups	**flour,** divided
10 cups plus 1 tablespoon	**water,** divided
²/₃ cup	**baking soda**
1	**egg yolk**
	coarse salt

In a small saucepan over medium-low, heat beer to 110 degrees; remove from heat. Stir in yeast until dissolved. In a large bowl, combine butter, sugar, salt, beer mixture, and 3 cups flour; beat until smooth. Stir in just enough remaining flour to form a soft dough. Knead on a floured surface until smooth and elastic, 6–8 minutes. Place in a greased bowl, turn once, cover with plastic wrap, and let rise in a warm place until doubled in size, about 1 hour.

Preheat oven to 425 degrees. Prepare a baking sheet with nonstick cooking spray. Punch dough down. Turn onto a lightly floured surface; divide and shape into 8 balls. Roll each ball in a 24-inch long rope and form in a pretzel shape, pinching ends to seal. In a large stockpot, bring 10 cups water and baking soda to a boil. Drop pretzels, 2 at a time, into boiling water. Cook 30 seconds. Remove with a slotted spoon; drain well on paper towels.

Place pretzels 2 inches apart on prepared baking sheet. In a small bowl, whisk together the egg yolk and 1 tablespoon water; brush over pretzels. Sprinkle with coarse salt. Bake 10–12 minutes, or until golden brown. Remove from pan to a wire rack to cool. Makes 8 large pretzels.

BEER AND PIMIENTO CHEESE MUFFINS

I can or bottle (12 ounces)	**beer,** room temperature
I jar (4 ounces)	**diced pimiento,** drained
I	**egg,** beaten
I teaspoon	**finely grated onion**
4 cups	**biscuit mix**
2 cups	**grated sharp cheddar cheese**

Preheat oven to 400 degrees. Prepare 18 muffin cups with nonstick cooking spray, or use paper liners.

In a large bowl, combine the beer, pimiento, egg, and onion. Add the biscuit mix and stir just until blended (batter may be lumpy). Stir in the cheese. Spoon batter into prepared muffin cups, filling them $^3/_4$ full.

Bake for 13–15 minutes, or until lightly browned. Remove from pan to a wire rack and let cool 10 minutes. Makes 18 muffins.

HONEY-WHEAT BEER BREAD

1 1/2 cups	**flour**
1 1/2 cups	**whole wheat flour**
4 1/2 teaspoons	**baking powder**
1 1/2 teaspoons	**salt**
1/3 cup	**packed light brown sugar**
1/4 cup plus 2 tablespoons	**honey,** divided
1 bottle (12 ounces)	**honey-wheat beer**
1/2 cup plus 1 tablespoon	**butter,** room temperature, divided

Preheat oven to 350 degrees. Lightly prepare a 9 x 5-inch loaf pan with nonstick cooking spray.

In a large bowl, combine flour, whole wheat flour, baking powder, salt, and brown sugar. Add 1/4 cup honey and the beer; stir until thoroughly blended. Pour into prepared loaf pan.

Melt 1 tablespoon butter in a small dish and add 1 tablespoon honey; mix. Brush the mixture over the bread and bake until top is golden brown and a toothpick inserted in the center comes out clean, about 50 minutes.

Combine the remaining 1/2 cup butter and remaining 1 tablespoon honey in a small bowl and stir until smooth; reserve. Remove the bread from the oven and cool for at least 15 minutes on a wire rack. Slice and serve with honey butter. Makes 1 loaf.

BEER CORNBREAD WAFFLES

1 1/2 cups	**flour**
1 1/2 cups	**yellow cornmeal**
1 tablespoon	**baking powder**
1 tablespoon	**sugar**
1 teaspoon	**salt**
1 cup	**whole milk**
3 tablespoons	**vegetable oil**
2	**eggs,** beaten
1 cup	**lager beer**
	butter and maple syrup

In a large bowl, whisk together flour, cornmeal, baking powder, sugar, and salt.

In a medium bowl, whisk together the milk, oil, and eggs until smooth. Stir into flour mixture until smooth. Gradually stir in beer just until incorporated; batter may be slightly lumpy. Rest for 5 minutes.

Coat a waffle iron with nonstick cooking spray and preheat. Add about 1/3 cup batter to waffle iron, spreading batter to edges. Cook until waffle is lightly browned and crispy; repeat with remaining batter. Serve warm waffles with butter and maple syrup. Makes about 12 waffles.

CHEESE AND CHIVE BEER SCONES

2³/₄ cups	**flour**
1 tablespoon	**sugar**
2 teaspoons	**baking powder**
1 teaspoon	**salt**
1 ¹/₂ cups	**grated cheddar cheese**
¹/₃ cup	**finely chopped fresh chives or minced green onion tops**
1 cup (or more)	**cold lager beer**
2	**eggs,** divided
1 tablespoon	**vegetable oil**
2 teaspoons	**Dijon mustard**
1 teaspoon	**water**

Preheat oven to 425 degrees. Line a baking sheet with parchment paper.

In a large bowl, whisk together the flour, sugar, baking powder, and salt. Stir in cheese and chives. Whisk the beer, 1 egg, oil, and mustard together in a small bowl. Gradually add beer mixture to dry ingredients, mixing until moist clumps form. (If dough is too dry, add more beer by tablespoonfuls, stirring after each addition.) Turn dough out on a lightly floured surface and knead just until dough comes together.

Pat the dough into a smooth disk about ³/₄ inch thick and transfer to the prepared baking sheet. Use a sharp knife to cut the disk into 8 wedges, spreading the wedges apart on the pan. Whisk remaining egg and water in a small dish, and brush over scones

Bake scones until golden on top and a toothpick inserted into center comes out clean, about 18–20 minutes. Cool on baking sheet for 5 minutes. Makes 8 scones.

BEER FOCACCIA BREAD

4 cups	**flour,** divided
1 tablespoon	**sugar**
2 tablespoons	**chopped fresh rosemary or 2 teaspoons dried rosemary,** divided
1 package (2 1/4 teaspoons)	**rapid rise yeast**
1 can or bottle (12 ounces)	**lager beer**
1/4 cup plus 2 tablespoons	**olive oil,** divided
1	**teaspoon salt**
2 teaspoons	**coarse salt**

Lightly prepare a 9 x 13-inch baking pan with nonstick cooking spray.

In the bowl of a stand mixer fitted with a dough hook, add 2 cups flour, sugar, 1 tablespoon fresh or 1 teaspoon dried rosemary, and yeast.

Pour the beer in a small saucepan and heat to 125 degrees. Add the beer to the mixer, and mix on medium speed until combined. Add the remaining 2 cups flour, 1/4 cup olive oil, and 1 teaspoon salt. Turn the mixer to medium-high and beat for 5–6 minutes. Transfer dough to a lightly oiled bowl, cover and allow to rise in a warm area until doubled in size, about 1 hour. Place dough in the prepared pan, and stretch to cover the entire pan. Cover and allow to rise for 30 minutes.

Preheat oven to 375 degrees. Press your fingers into the dough to make indentations across the entire pan. Drizzle with the remaining 2 tablespoons olive oil, and sprinkle with the remaining 1 tablespoon fresh or 1 teaspoon dried rosemary, and coarse salt. Bake until golden brown, about 25–30 minutes. Makes 1 loaf.

GERMAN COFFEE CAKE

2 cups	**packed dark brown sugar**
1 cup	**butter,** softened
2	**eggs**
1 teaspoon	**cinnamon**
$^1/_2$ teaspoon	**allspice**
$^1/_2$ teaspoon	**ground cloves**
3 cups plus 1 tablespoon	**flour,** divided
2 teaspoons	**baking soda**
$^1/_2$ teaspoon	**salt**
2 cups	**beer**
2 cups	**chopped dates**
1 cup	**chopped walnuts**
	powdered sugar

Preheat oven to 350 degrees. Prepare a large Bundt pan with nonstick cooking spray and dust with flour.

In a large bowl, combine brown sugar and butter. Beat until smooth and well-blended. Add the eggs, one at a time, beating well after each addition.

In a medium bowl, whisk together cinnamon, allspice, cloves, 3 cups flour, baking soda, and salt. Add $^1/_2$ of the flour mixture alternated with $^1/_2$ of the beer to creamed mixture, blending well after each addition; repeat. Sprinkle the dates with the remaining 1 tablespoon flour. Stir walnuts and dates into batter, and pour evenly into prepared pan.

Bake for 1$^1/_4$ hours, or until a toothpick inserted into the center comes out clean. Let stand 5 minutes before inverting onto a wire rack. Sprinkle with powdered sugar and transfer to a serving plate. Makes 10 servings.

BEST GLAZED BANANA BREAD

1 $^3/_4$ cups	**flour**
$^3/_4$ cup	**sugar**
1 $^1/_4$ teaspoons	**baking powder**
$^1/_2$ teaspoon	**baking soda**
1 teaspoon	**cinnamon**
$^3/_4$ teaspoon	**salt**
2	**eggs**
2	**ripe bananas,** mashed
$^1/_3$ cup	**butter,** melted
$^1/_2$ cup	**beer,** divided
$^1/_2$ cup	**chopped walnuts**
2 cups	**powdered sugar**
1 tablespoon	**corn syrup**

Preheat oven to 325 degrees. Lightly prepare a 9 x 5-inch loaf pan with nonstick cooking spray.

In a medium bowl, whisk together the flour, sugar, baking powder, baking soda, cinnamon, and salt. In a large bowl, whisk the eggs until frothy. Add the bananas, butter, $^1/_4$ cup beer, and mix well. Add the flour mixture and stir just until combined. Fold in the walnuts and spread into the prepared pan, smoothing the top. Let rest for 10 minutes.

Bake for 45 minutes. Remove from oven and lay a piece of aluminum foil across the top to prevent over-browning. Return to oven and bake for an additional 25 minutes, or until a toothpick inserted into the center comes out clean. Cool in pan for 15 minutes. Arrange a wire rack over a baking sheet, remove bread from the pan and transfer to the rack; cool to room temperature.

In a small dish, whisk together the powdered sugar, corn syrup, and remaining $^1/_4$ cup beer. Drizzle the glaze over the bread and let sit or 30 minutes before slicing. Makes 1 loaf.

SAUCES AND CONDIMENTS

BEER BARBECUE SAUCE

I cup	**ketchup**
I cup	**regular or non-alcoholic beer**
I can (6 ounces)	**tomato paste**
$1/3$ cup	**maple syrup**
3 tablespoons	**cider vinegar**
3 tablespoons	**mustard**
I tablespoon	**Worcestershire sauce**
$2/3$ cup	**packed light brown sugar**
2 teaspoons	**salt**
2 teaspoons	**dry mustard**
2 teaspoons	**garlic powder**
2 teaspoons	**onion powder**
I teaspoon	**dried oregano**
I teaspoon	**pepper**
I teaspoon	**paprika**
$1/4$ teaspoon	**cayenne pepper**

In a large pot over medium heat, combine the ketchup, beer, tomato paste, maple syrup, vinegar, mustard, and Worcestershire sauce; stir to combine.

In a medium bowl, whisk together the brown sugar, salt, mustard, garlic powder, onion powder, oregano, pepper, paprika, and cayenne pepper. Add to the beer mixture and whisk until smooth.

Increase the heat to medium-high and cook, stirring constantly, until mixture comes to a boil. Reduce heat to low and simmer for 5 minutes. Remove from heat and cool for 15 minutes before serving. Store in the refrigerator in a tightly covered container for up to I month. Makes about 4 cups.

BEER CHEDDAR SAUCE

8 ounces	**cream cheese,** softened
I cup	**wheat beer**
I teaspoon	**Worcestershire sauce**
8 ounces	**cheddar cheese,** grated
8 ounces	**mozzarella cheese,** grated
2 cloves	**garlic,** peeled and minced

Melt the cream cheese in a large saucepan over medium heat. Add the beer and Worcestershire sauce, and stir until combined. Add the cheddar cheese, mozzarella cheese, and garlic. Heat, stirring constantly, until cheeses melt and mixture is smooth. Serve over hot cooked noodles, potatoes, or chicken. Makes about 3 $1/2$ cups or 8 servings.

BEST BEER TURKEY BRINE

3 cans or bottles (12 ounces each)	**regular or non-alcoholic beer**
4 cups	**turkey or chicken stock or broth**
2 cups	**kosher salt**
$^1/_2$ cup	**sugar**
$^1/_2$ cup	**packed light brown sugar**
4	**bay leaves,** crumbled
1 tablespoon	**whole black peppercorns**
4 quarts	**ice water**

Mix beer, stock, salt, sugar, brown sugar, bay leaves, and peppercorns in a large, lidded, stainless steel or enamel 20-quart stockpot. Cook uncovered over medium heat, stirring occasionally, until salt and sugar are dissolved, about 15 minutes. Remove from heat and add the ice water; stir until ice is melted. Place turkey in brine and weight the lid to keep it submerged. Refrigerate 12–24 hours.

Remove turkey from brine and pat dry. Discard remaining brine and roast as usual. Makes enough brine for a 12–14 pound turkey. If brining a larger turkey, multiply the brine recipe accordingly so the turkey is entirely submerged in the brine before chilling.

STOUT MUSHROOM SAUCE

2 tablespoons	**olive oil**
2	**medium shallots,** peeled and finely chopped
2 cloves	**garlic,** peeled and minced
1 pound	**mushrooms,** trimmed and quartered
1 cup	**stout beer,** such as Guinness
2 teaspoons	**balsamic vinegar**
1 teaspoon	**sugar**
$^1/_2$ teaspoon	**salt**

Heat the olive oil in a frying pan over medium heat until it shimmers. Add the shallots and cook until transparent, about 3 minutes. Add the garlic and stir. Add the mushrooms and cook, stirring occasionally, until lightly browned, about 5 minutes.

Increase the heat to medium-high and slowly add the beer, stirring until mixture stops foaming. Add the vinegar, sugar, and salt; stir to combine. Cook until mixture starts to simmer. Reduce heat to medium and cook until liquid is reduced by half, about 10 minutes, stirring occasionally. Remove from heat and serve with steaks, roasted chicken, or pork chops. Makes about 3 cups or 6 servings.

SPICY BEER MUSTARD

$1/3$ cup	**yellow mustard seeds**
$1/4$ cup	**brown mustard seeds**
$1/2$ cup	**cider vinegar**
1 cup	**dark beer,** divided
3 tablespoons	**packed dark brown sugar**
2 tablespoons	**honey**
1 teaspoon	**salt**
$1/2$ teaspoon	**turmeric**
$1/8$ teaspoon	**allspice**

In a small bowl, cover the yellow and brown mustard seeds with vinegar and $1/2$ cup of beer. Cover and place in the refrigerator overnight.

In a small saucepan, mix together remaining $1/2$ cup beer, sugar, honey, salt, turmeric, and allspice. Bring to a boil over medium heat, remove from heat, and let cool slightly.

In the jar of a blender add mustard seeds with their soaking liquid and cooled mixture from saucepan. Puree until smooth. Transfer to a covered container and refrigerate at least 2 hours before serving. Mustard may be stored, tightly covered, for up to 3 months. Makes about $2 1/3$ cups.

ORANGE ALE
SALAD DRESSING

$1/4$ cup	**pale ale**
1	**small shallot,** peeled and minced
1 tablespoon	**orange juice**
1 tablespoon	**honey**
1 teaspoon	**finely grated orange zest**
1 teaspoon	**Dijon mustard**
$1/4$ teaspoon	**salt**
$1/8$ teaspoon	**pepper**
$1/4$ cup	**olive oil**

In a small bowl, whisk the beer with the shallot, orange juice, honey, orange zest, mustard, salt, and pepper. Gradually add the oil in a thin stream, whisking constantly. Serve at once or refrigerate up to 4 days. Makes about $2/3$ cup or 6 servings.

APPLE ALE GINGER CHUTNEY

I tablespoon	**vegetable oil**
I	**large yellow onion,** chopped
I tablespoon	**finely grated fresh ginger**
$^1/_4$ cup	**apple cider vinegar**
3	**large Granny Smith apples,** peeled, cored, and chopped
$^1/_2$ teaspoon	**cinnamon**
$^1/_2$ teaspoon	**nutmeg**
2 cups	**ale**
$^1/_4$ cup	**packed dark brown sugar**
I tablespoon	**lemon juice**
$^1/_2$ teaspoon	**salt**

Heat oil in a medium saucepan over medium heat. Add the onion and cook, stirring occasionally, until softened, about 5 minutes. Add the ginger and vinegar and cook, stirring constantly, for I minute. Add the apples, cinnamon, nutmeg, ale, brown sugar, lemon juice, and salt. Reduce heat to medium-low, and cook for about 30 minutes, or until liquid is almost gone. Remove from heat, and cool for 10 minutes before serving. Refrigerate in a tightly covered container for up to 10 days. Makes about $3^1/_2$ cups.

BEER BUTTERSCOTCH SAUCE

2 cups	**sugar**
$^1/_2$ cup	**red or brown ale**
8 tablespoons	**butter,** softened, cut into cubes
1 cup	**heavy cream,** room temperature
$^1/_2$ teaspoon	**salt**

In a medium saucepan over medium-high heat, combine the sugar and ale and cook, stirring, until sugar dissolves. Bring to a boil and continue cooking, without stirring, until mixture turns deep amber in color and a candy thermometer registers 350 degrees.

Quickly add the butter and stir constantly until butter melts. Remove from heat and slowly whisk in cream until completely incorporated. Add the salt and stir. Cool for 10 minutes before serving. Store in the refrigerator in a tightly covered container for up to 10 days. Makes about 3 $^1/_2$ cups.

SOUPS

BEST BEER CHEESE SOUP

4 tablespoons	**butter**
1	**small onion,** chopped
1	**large carrot,** peeled and diced
2 stalks	**celery,** diced
3 cloves	**garlic,** peeled and minced
$^1/_4$ cup	**flour**
3 cups	**chicken stock or broth**
1 can or bottle (12 ounces)	**regular or non-alcoholic beer**
4 ounces	**cream cheese,** softened
8 ounces	**sharp cheddar cheese,** grated
8 ounces	**Colby cheese,** grated
1 cup	**half-and-half**
1 teaspoon	**Dijon mustard**
$^1/_4$ teaspoon	**Worcestershire sauce**
	salt and pepper, to taste

In a large pot, melt the butter over medium heat. Add the onion, carrot, and celery, and cook until softened, about 8 minutes. Add the garlic and cook for 1 minute.

Sprinkle in the flour and cook, stirring constantly, until smooth and slightly thickened, about 2 minutes. Whisk in the chicken stock and beer, and bring just to a boil. Reduce heat and simmer, uncovered, stirring occasionally, 40–45 minutes. Strain through a fine mesh sieve, and reserve vegetables.

Return beer mixture back to the Dutch oven and bring to a simmer over medium-low heat. Add the cream cheese and stir until melted and smooth. Add the cheeses $^1/_3$ cup at a time, whisking after each addition until cheese melts. Stir in the half-and-half, Dijon mustard, and Worcestershire sauce, and heat to simmering. Stir in the reserved vegetables and season with salt and pepper. Makes 8 servings.

CREAMY CRAB CHOWDER

4 tablespoons	**butter**
1	**onion,** chopped
3 stalks	**celery,** diced
1	**medium potato,** peeled and diced
2 cloves	**garlic,** peeled and minced
3 tablespoons	**flour**
4 cups	**chicken stock or broth**
$1/2$ pound	**Monterey Jack cheese,** cut in $1/4$-inch cubes
1 can or bottle (12 ounces)	**regular or non-alcoholic beer**
1 pound	**crab meat,** picked through for shells
1 cup	**heavy cream**
1 tablespoon	**chopped fresh parsley**
1 teaspoon	**Worcestershire sauce**
	salt and pepper, to taste

In a large pot, melt the butter and cook the onion, celery, potato, and garlic for 3 minutes over medium heat. Sprinkle in the flour and stir to combine. Add chicken stock and simmer 10 minutes on low heat. Add cheese and beer, and simmer until vegetables are tender and cheese is fully melted. Add crab meat, cream, parsley, and Worcestershire sauce and cook for 5 minutes. Season with salt and pepper. Makes 8 servings.

BEER AND BACON SPLIT PEA SOUP

1/2 pound	**bacon,** diced
I	**large carrot,** peeled and finely chopped
I	**medium onion,** finely chopped
2 cloves	**garlic,** peeled and minced
2 cups	**green split peas,** rinsed and picked through for small stones
3 1/2 cups	**chicken stock or broth**
I can or bottle (12 ounces)	**regular or non-alcoholic beer**
	salt and pepper, to taste
	minced green onion

In a large pot over medium-low heat, cook the bacon until it just begins to brown, about 7–10 minutes. Add the carrot and onion and cook until carrots soften and onion is translucent, about 5–7 minutes. Add the garlic and cook, stirring, for I minute.

Add the split peas, chicken stock, and beer and bring to a simmer. Cover and simmer, stirring occasionally, until peas are tender and soup is thick, about 2 hours; add water if needed to keep peas covered. Season with salt and pepper and garnish with green onion before serving. Makes 6 servings.

FRENCH APPLE
AND BRIE SOUP

2 tablespoons	**olive oil**
1	**sweet onion,** such as Vidalia, chopped
$^2/_3$ cup	**apple cider or juice**
3	**medium apples,** peeled, cored, and chopped
1 can or bottle (12 ounces)	**light beer**
2 cups	**chicken stock or broth**
$^1/_4$ teaspoon	**cayenne pepper**
$^1/_4$ cup	**flour**
1 cup	**whole milk**
1 pound	**Brie cheese,** rind removed, cut in $^1/_2$-inch cubes
8 ounces	**sharp cheddar cheese,** finely grated
	salt and white pepper, to taste

Heat the olive oil in a large pot over medium heat. Add the onion and cook, until softened, about 5 minutes. Add the apple cider and cook, stirring frequently, until mixture starts to simmer, about 4 minutes. Add the apples and cook until softened, 8 minutes. Add the beer, chicken broth, and cayenne. Bring to a simmer and cook, stirring occasionally, until apples are tender, 7–10 minutes.

In a small bowl, whisk the flour and milk together until smooth; reserve. Take the soup off the heat and transfer half of it into a food processor or blender. Puree until smooth, return to the pot, and heat to simmering. Whisk in the milk mixture and heat until mixture bubbles; cook until soup thickens slightly, about 5 minutes. Stir in the Brie a handful at a time, until melted and smooth. Stir in the cheddar cheese and cook, stirring, just until melted. Season with salt and pepper. Makes 6–8 servings.

TEXAS RED CHILI

3 tablespoons	**vegetable oil**
3 pounds	**flank steak,** cut in $^1/_2$-inch cubes
I	**medium onion,** finely chopped
I $^3/_4$ cups	**beef stock or broth**
I can or bottle (I2 ounces)	**regular or non-alcoholic beer**
I can (8 ounces)	**tomato sauce**
I tablespoon	**tomato paste**
I teaspoon	**hot pepper sauce**
$^1/_4$ cup	**chili powder**
I tablespoon	**cumin**
I teaspoon	**garlic powder**
	salt and pepper, to taste

Heat the oil in a large pot over medium heat and cook the steak and onion, stirring occasionally, until lightly browned. Add the beef stock and bring to a simmer. Add the beer, tomato sauce, tomato paste, hot pepper sauce, chili powder, cumin, and garlic powder; stir to combine. Bring mixture to a simmer and cook for 2 hours stirring occasionally. Season with salt and pepper. Makes I2 servings.

IRISH RED POTATO SOUP

2 pounds	**red potatoes,** cut in $1/2$-inch cubes
I	**small onion,** chopped
2 cups	**chicken stock or broth**
I can or bottle (12 ounces)	**regular or non-alcoholic beer**
I cup	**half-and-half**
$1/2$ teaspoon	**salt**
$1/2$ teaspoon	**dry mustard**
$1/2$ teaspoon	**white pepper**
2 cups	**grated cheddar cheese**
4 slices	**bacon,** cooked and crumbled

Combine the potatoes, onion, and chicken stock in a large saucepan over medium-high heat and bring to a boil. Reduce heat to medium-low, cover and simmer until potatoes are tender, about 15–20 minutes.

Stir in the beer, half-and-half, salt, mustard, and white pepper, and bring to a simmer. Add the cheese a handful at a time, stirring after each addition until cheese is melted. When all the cheese is incorporated, remove from heat and adjust seasonings, if necessary. Garnish with crumbled bacon. Makes 8 servings.

CHICKEN WILD RICE SOUP

1	**onion,** diced
3	**medium carrots,** peeled and diced
3 stalks	**celery,** diced
4	**boneless, skinless chicken breasts,** diced
2 cups	**wild rice blend,** rinsed and drained
6 1/2 cups	**chicken stock or broth**
2 cans or bottles (12 ounces each)	**wheat beer**
1 teaspoon	**salt**
1/2 teaspoon	**pepper**
1/2 teaspoon	**dried thyme**
4 ounces	**cream cheese,** softened
8 ounces	**extra sharp cheddar cheese,** grated
	flat-leaf parsley, chopped

Combine the onion, carrots, celery, chicken, wild rice blend, chicken stock, beer, salt, pepper, and thyme in a 6-quart slow cooker. Stir well, cover, and cook on low for 7 hours.

Add the cream cheese and cheddar cheese and continue cooking, stirring occasionally, until the cheeses are completely melted. Serve soup topped with chopped fresh parsley. Makes 8–10 servings.

SLOW COOKER BEER 'N' BRATWURST CHEDDAR SOUP

I	**medium yellow onion,** finely diced
4	**large carrots,** peeled and finely diced
4 cups	**chicken stock or broth**
2 cloves	**garlic,** peeled and minced
I tablespoon	**Dijon mustard**
I can or bottle (12 ounces)	**regular or non-alcoholic beer**
2 packages (19.2 ounces each)	**pre-cooked bratwursts,** cut in $1/4$-inch slices
2 pounds	**processed American cheese,** cut in $1/2$-inch cubes
I pound	**sharp cheddar cheese,** finely grated
	chopped parsley

In a 6-quart slow cooker, combine the onion, carrots, chicken stock, garlic, mustard, beer, and bratwurst. Cover and cook on low for 6 hours. Add processed cheese, cover and cook an additional hour until the cheese is fully melted. Stir in the cheddar cheese and serve garnished with parsley. Makes 10 servings.

FRENCH ONION SOUP

6 tablespoons	**butter,** softened, divided
2 tablespoons	**olive oil**
4	**large onions,** sliced
2 cans or bottles (12 ounces each)	**dark beer**
4 cups	**chicken stock or broth**
2 1/2 cups	**beef stock or broth**
I tablespoon	**Worcestershire sauce**
2 cloves	**garlic,** peeled and minced
	salt and pepper, to taste
8 (1 1/2 inch) slices	**French bread**
6 ounces	**Gruyere or Swiss cheese,** grated

Heat 2 tablespoons of butter and olive oil in a large pot over medium-low heat. Add onions and cook for 5 minutes. Reduce heat to low and continue cooking, stirring occasionally, until onions become deep golden brown, 45–60 minutes. Add the beer, chicken stock, beef stock, Worcestershire Sauce, and garlic and reduce heat to low. Simmer for 45 minutes; season with salt and pepper.

Preheat the oven broiler to low. Butter one side of the 8 bread slices with the remaining 4 tablespoons of butter, arrange on a baking sheet, and broil until brown and crispy. Arrange 8 broiler-safe bowls or crocks on a large baking sheet. Ladle the soup in the bowls, filling about halfway, and place I piece of toasted bread in each bowl. Sprinkle with cheese and broil until cheese is melted and bubbly, 2–3 minutes. Makes 8 servings.

BEER BEEF STEW

3 tablespoons	**olive oil**
1 tablespoon	**butter**
2 pounds	**beef chuck,** cut in $1/2$-inch cubes
3 cloves	**garlic,** peeled and minced
1	**medium onion,** diced
1 can or bottle (12 ounces)	**dark beer**
4 cups	**beef stock or broth,** more as needed
1 tablespoon	**Worcestershire sauce**
2–3 tablespoons	**tomato paste**
$1/2$ teaspoon	**paprika**
$1/2$ teaspoon	**salt**
$1/4$ teaspoon	**pepper**
3	**carrots,** peeled and cut in $1/4$-inch slices
1	**large turnip,** peeled and diced
2 tablespoons	**flour**
	flat-leaf parsley, chopped

Heat the oil and butter in a large pot over medium-high heat. Cook the beef until browned on all sides, about 6–8 minutes. Remove beef from pot and drain on paper towels. Add the garlic and onion to the pot and cook until softened, about 3 minutes. Add the beer, beef stock, Worcestershire sauce, tomato paste, paprika, salt, and pepper. Return the beef to the pot, cover and simmer on a low heat until the meat is very tender, $1 1/2$ –2 hours. If the liquid level gets too low, add additional water as needed.

Add the carrots and turnips and continue to simmer until the vegetables are tender and the liquid is reduced, about 30 minutes.

Remove 1 cup of cooking liquid from the pan and stir in the flour. Add the flour mixture back into the pot and stir. Simmer until the stew is thick, about 10 minutes. Garnish with chopped parsley. Makes 8 servings.

BACON CHEESEBURGER SOUP

$^3/_4$ pound	**sliced bacon,** chopped
I pound	**lean ground beef**
$^1/_4$ cup	**flour**
2 teaspoons	**paprika**
I teaspoon	**seasoning salt**
$^1/_2$ teaspoon	**onion powder**
$^1/_2$ teaspoon	**pepper**
I can or bottle (12 ounces)	**regular or non-alcoholic beer**
4 cups	**half-and-half**
I pound	**mild cheddar cheese,** grated
$^1/_2$ cup	**croutons**
2	**large dill pickles,** chopped

In a large pot, cook the bacon over medium-high heat until just crisp, stirring often. Drain off most of the fat and add the ground beef to the pot. Break up the meat and cook until no longer pink, stirring occasionally, about 6 minutes. Pour off all but 2 tablespoons of pan drippings.

Sprinkle the flour, paprika, seasoning salt, onion powder, and pepper over the meat. Cook, stirring constantly, for 2 minutes. Add the beer and cook, stirring, for 3 minutes. Stir in the half-and-half and cook until mixture simmers. Add cheese and cook, stirring constantly, until cheese is completely melted. Cook for 5 more minutes, stirring constantly. Remove from heat and cool for 5 minutes before serving. Garnish with croutons and chopped pickles. Makes 8 servings.

NAVY BEAN, SMOKED SAUSAGE, AND BEER SOUP

I pound	**dried navy beans,** rinsed and picked through for small stones
4 1/2 cups	**chicken stock or broth**
I can or bottle (12 ounces)	**regular or non-alcoholic beer**
I can (15 ounces)	**diced tomatoes,** with liquid
I	**onion,** chopped
2 stalks	**celery,** chopped
3 cloves	**garlic,** peeled and minced
I pound	**smoked sausage links,** cut in 1/2-inch slices
2 tablespoons	**Worcestershire sauce**
I	**bay leaf**
	salt and pepper, to taste
	flat-leaf parsley, chopped

Combine beans, chicken stock, beer, tomatoes, onion, celery, garlic, smoked sausage, Worcestershire sauce, and bay leaf in a large pot; heat over medium-high until mixture comes to a boil. Lower heat, cover, and simmer for 4 hours, or until beans are tender, stirring occasionally and adding water if mixture becomes too thick. Season with salt and pepper, discarding bay leaf before serving. Garnish with chopped parsley. Makes 8 servings.

DINNERS

ONE-PAN
BEER ONION CHICKEN

¹/₄ cup	**flour,** divided
1 (3–4 pound)	**broiler/fryer chicken,** cut in pieces,* skin removed
2 tablespoons	**olive oil**
1 envelope (1 ounce)	**onion soup mix**
1 can or bottle (12 ounces)	**regular or non-alcoholic beer**

Place 2 tablespoons flour in a large ziplock bag. Add chicken, a few pieces at a time, and shake to coat.

Heat the olive oil in a large frying pan over medium-high heat until it shimmers. Cook the chicken pieces in batches until browned on all sides. Remove and drain on paper towels; keep warm.

Add soup mix and remaining flour to frying pan, stirring to loosen browned bits from the bottom. Gradually whisk in beer. Bring to a boil; cook and stir for 2 minutes, or until thickened. Return chicken pieces to the pan and bring mixture to a boil. Reduce heat; cover and simmer for 12–15 minutes, or until chicken is cooked through and an instant-read thermometer registers 170 degrees. Makes 6 servings.

*Your butcher or grocer's meat department can cut up a whole chicken, or you can use 3–4 pounds of your favorite chicken pieces.

BEER BACON MAC AND CHEESE

1 package (16 ounces)	**elbow macaroni**
1/4 cup	**butter**
2 cloves	**garlic,** peeled and minced
3 tablespoons	**flour**
2 teaspoons	**dry mustard**
1 teaspoon	**salt**
3/4 teaspoon	**pepper**
2 1/2 cups	**milk**
3/4 cup	**regular or non-alcoholic light beer**
1/4 cup	**heavy cream**
3 cups	**grated cheddar cheese,** divided
2 cups	**grated Gruyère cheese**
2 tablespoons	**grated Parmesan cheese,** divided
2	**green onions,** minced
6 slices	**bacon,** cooked and crumbled

Preheat oven to 400 degrees. Prepare a 3-quart baking dish with nonstick cooking spray. Cook macaroni according to package directions; drain and set aside.

In a large saucepan, melt the butter over medium heat. Add the garlic; cook and stir for 1 minute. Stir in the flour, mustard, salt, and pepper until smooth; gradually whisk in the milk, beer, and cream. Bring to a boil; cook and stir for 2 minutes, or until thickened. Reduce heat and stir in 2 cups of the cheddar cheese, Gruyère cheese, and 1 tablespoon Parmesan cheese until melted. Add green onions. Stir macaroni into sauce and transfer to prepared baking dish; sprinkle remaining cheddar and Parmesan cheese over top. Bake, uncovered, for 15–20 minutes, or until golden brown and heated through. Top with crumbled bacon and let stand for 5 minutes before serving. Makes 8–10 servings.

BEER-INATED GRILLED PORK CHOPS

I can or bottle (12 ounces)	**beer**
I tablespoon	**balsamic vinegar**
3 tablespoons	**maple syrup**
2 tablespoons	**prepared mustard**
2 cloves	**garlic,** peeled and minced
2 teaspoons	**salt**
I teaspoon	**pepper**
$1/2$ teaspoon	**dried sage**
I	**small onion,** sliced
8 (1-inch thick)	**center-cut pork chops**
	vegetable oil

In a medium bowl, whisk together the beer, vinegar, maple syrup, mustard, garlic, salt, pepper, and sage. Pour mixture into a 1-gallon ziplock bag. Add the onion and pork chops, coat with the marinade, squeeze out excess air, and seal the bag. Marinate in the refrigerator for 8–12 hours, turning several times.

Preheat the grill to medium heat and lightly oil the grate. Remove the pork chops from the marinade and pat dry; discard the marinade. Cook the pork chops until an instant-read thermometer inserted in the center reads 145 degrees, about 7 minutes per side. Makes 8 servings.

BEER CHEESE FONDUE

2 tablespoons	**flour**
$^1/_2$ teaspoon	**salt**
$^1/_4$ teaspoon	**pepper**
2 cups	**grated sharp cheddar cheese**
2 cups	**grated Swiss cheese**
1 clove	**garlic,** peeled
1 can or bottle (12 ounces)	**regular or non-alcoholic beer**
3 drops	**hot pepper sauce**
	assorted raw vegetables
	French bread, cut in 1 $^1/_2$-inch cubes

In a medium bowl, combine flour, salt, and pepper. Add the cheddar and Swiss cheese, and toss with a fork to coat the cheeses with the flour mixture. Cut the garlic clove in half and rub it around the bottom and sides of a fondue pot or heavy-bottomed saucepan. Pour beer into fondue pot and slowly bring to a simmer over medium-low heat, about 5 minutes. Gradually add cheese mixture to beer, stirring after each addition until cheese is melted and blended. Add hot pepper sauce and stir until smooth. Serve fondue warm with vegetables and French bread cubes. Makes 6 servings.

BEER-SIMMERED SAUSAGE AND RICE

2 cups	**white rice**
4 cups	**chicken stock or broth**
2 tablespoons	**vegetable oil**
I pound	**smoked sausage,** cut in $^1/_4$-inch slices
I clove	**garlic,** peeled and minced
I	**large onion,** chopped
I stalk	**celery,** chopped
I	**medium red bell pepper,** seeded and chopped
	salt and pepper, to taste
I cup	**regular or non-alcoholic beer**
$^1/_4$ teaspoon	**cayenne pepper**
$^1/_4$ cup	**chopped flat-leaf parsley**

Combine the rice and chicken stock in a medium saucepan and bring to a boil over medium-high heat. Reduce heat to medium-low, cover and simmer until all the stock is absorbed into the rice, about 20 minutes.

Heat oil in a frying pan over medium-high heat and cook the sausage, stirring occasionally, until lightly browned. Add the garlic, onion, celery, and bell pepper, and cook until softened, about 5 minutes. Season with salt and pepper. Add the beer and cayenne pepper and cook, stirring occasionally, for 10 minutes. Add the cooked rice and parsley and cook for 5 minutes, stirring constantly. Adjust seasonings, if necessary, and serve. Makes 6 servings.

BEER BARBECUE SLOW COOKER RIBS

3 pounds	**bone-in pork spareribs,** cut in individual ribs
3 tablespoons	**liquid smoke flavoring**
2 tablespoons	**packed dark brown sugar**
1 tablespoon	**chili powder**
2 teaspoons	**paprika**
1 teaspoon	**garlic powder**
$1/2$ teaspoon	**salt**
$1/2$ teaspoon	**pepper**
1 can or bottle (12 ounces)	**regular or non-alcoholic beer**
2 cups	**barbecue sauce**

Trim any excess fat from the ribs and remove the membrane. Arrange the ribs on a baking sheet and brush all sides with the liquid smoke flavoring. In a small bowl, combine the brown sugar, chili powder, paprika, garlic powder, salt, and pepper. Rub the mixture all over the ribs. Pour the beer in a 6-quart slow cooker and arrange the ribs inside. Cover and cook on low for 6 hours.

Preheat the grill to medium-high heat and lightly oil the grill grate. Remove the ribs from the slow cooker and allow them to rest for 10 minutes. Brush ribs with barbecue sauce and place on grill, turning once, until lightly browned, about 6–8 minutes. Transfer to a serving platter and brush with more barbecue sauce. Makes 4–6 servings.

BEER BOILED SHRIMP

3 cans or bottles (12 ounces each)	**regular or non-alcoholic beer**
1 1/2 cups	**water**
2 tablespoons	**seafood seasoning**
2 teaspoons	**lemon juice**
3 cloves	**garlic,** peeled and minced
1/2 teaspoon	**dried dill**
1/2 teaspoon	**pepper**
3 pounds	**large tail-on shrimp**
1 1/2	**cups cocktail sauce**
	fresh lemon wedges

In a large pot over medium-high heat, combine the beer, water, seafood seasoning, lemon juice, garlic, dill, and pepper; bring to a boil. Boil for 5 minutes, stirring occasionally. Add shrimp, cover, and simmer for 3 minutes. Remove lid and stir to redistribute shrimp. Cover and cook until shrimp turn pink, about 3–4 minutes. Drain liquid and serve warm with cocktail sauce and lemon wedges. Makes 6 servings.

BEEF AND STOUT POTPIE

2 tablespoons	**olive oil**
1 pound	**beef chuck steak,** cut in 1-inch cubes
2 slices	**bacon,** chopped
1	**onion,** chopped
1	**carrot,** peeled and sliced
1/3 pound	**mushrooms,** sliced
1 clove	**garlic,** peeled and crushed
1 1/2 tablespoons	**flour**
1 cup	**stout beer,** such as Guinness
1 1/4 cups	**beef stock or broth**
1/2 teaspoon	**dried thyme**
2	**bay leaves**
1 teaspoon	**cornstarch**
2 teaspoons	**warm water**
1 sheet	**frozen puff pastry,** thawed
1	**egg,** beaten

Heat oil in a large pot over medium heat, and brown the beef on all sides, remove to a plate; reserve. Add bacon to the pot and cook over medium heat just until it begins to brown. Add the onion, carrot, mushrooms, and garlic and cook, stirring occasionally, until tender, about 10 minutes. Sprinkle the flour over the mixture and stir to incorporate. Add the beer, beef stock, thyme, bay leaves, and reserved beef. Bring to a boil, reduce heat to a simmer, and cover and cook until tender, about 1 hour and 15 minutes, stirring occasionally. Increase heat to medium, uncover and cook for 15 minutes. In a small bowl, whisk together the cornstarch and water. Stir mixture into the stew and simmer for 30 minutes, stirring occasionally. Remove from heat and discard bay leaves. Preheat oven to 350 degrees. Pour stew in a 9-inch glass pie dish. Cut the puff pastry in a 10-inch circle, and place on top of the filling. Crimp the edges around the dish and make 3 1-inch cuts in the top of the pastry. Brush the pastry with the beaten egg. Bake until crust is browned, 30–40 minutes. Makes 4–6 servings.

CHICKEN AND DUMPLINGS

2 pounds	**boneless, skinless chicken breasts**
2 teaspoons	**salt,** divided
$^1/_2$ teaspoon	**pepper**
2 tablespoons	**vegetable oil**
1	**large onion,** chopped
2 stalks	**celery,** thinly sliced
2	**medium carrots,** peeled and thinly sliced
1 clove	**garlic,** peeled and minced
2 cups plus 1 tablespoon	**flour,** divided
1 can or bottle (12 ounces)	**beer**
$^1/_2$ teaspoon	**dried thyme**
2 cups	**chicken stock or broth**
1	**bay leaf**
2 teaspoons	**baking powder**
2 tablespoons	**butter,** melted
$^3/_4$ cup	**milk**

Season the chicken with 1 teaspoon salt and pepper. Heat the oil in a large pot over medium-high heat. Cook the chicken until lightly browned, about 6 minutes. Transfer to a platter and keep warm. Add the onion, celery, and carrots to the top. Cook until soft, about 5 minutes, stirring constantly. Stir in the garlic and cook for 1 minute. Sprinkle 1 tablespoon flour over the mixture and cook for 30 seconds, stirring constantly. Add the beer, scraping up any browned bits from bottom of pan, and whisk until the mixture thickens. Stir in the thyme, chicken stock, and bay leaf, and bring to a simmer. Chop the chicken in 1-inch pieces and add to the pot; cover, reduce heat to low, and simmer for 15 minutes. In a medium bowl, whisk together 2 cups flour, baking powder, and 1 teaspoon salt. Add the butter and milk and stir just until combined. Remove the bay leaf from the pot. Drop the dough by rounded teaspoonfuls on top of the stew. Cover and cook on low for 15 minutes. Makes 6–8 servings.

WELSH RAREBIT

4 tablespoons	**butter**
$1/4$ cup	**flour**
$1/2$ teaspoon	**salt**
$1/4$ teaspoon	**pepper**
$1/4$ teaspoon	**dry mustard**
$1/4$ teaspoon	**Worcestershire sauce**
2 drops	**hot pepper sauce**
1 cup	**whole milk**
$1/2$ cup	**regular or non-alcoholic beer**
2 cups	**grated cheddar cheese**
6 slices	**bread,** toasted
6 ($1/4$-inch thick)	**tomato slices**

Melt the butter in a large saucepan over medium heat. Add the flour, salt, pepper, mustard, Worcestershire sauce, and hot pepper sauce and whisk to combine. Cook, stirring constantly, until the mixture is smooth and bubbling, about 5 minutes.

Remove from heat and slowly stir in the milk, whisking constantly. Return to heat and stir constantly until the mixture comes to a boil. Slowly pour in the beer and cook 1 minute more while still stirring. Add $1/4$ of the cheese and whisk until cheese is completely melted. Repeat process with remaining cheese, whisking after each addition.

To serve, arrange 1 slice of toast on each of 6 plates and top with a tomato slice. Ladle the sauce over the toast. Makes 6 servings.

BEER-SIMMERED CHICKEN TACOS

2 tablespoons	**vegetable oil**
1	**large onion,** finely chopped
1 clove	**garlic,** peeled and minced
2 cups	**shredded cooked chicken**
1 cup	**beer**
1 can (4 ounces)	**diced green chiles**
1 tablespoon	**chili powder**
$1/2$ teaspoon	**ground cumin**
$1/2$ teaspoon	**salt**
8	**crispy corn taco shells,** heated as directed on box
$1/2$ cup	**grated Mexican blend cheese**
$1/2$ cup	**sour cream**

In a large frying pan, heat oil over medium-high heat. Add onion and cook until transparent, about 5 minutes. Stir in garlic and cook for 1 minute. Add chicken, beer, green chiles, chili powder, cumin, and salt, and heat until mixture just starts to boil. Reduce heat to low and cook, uncovered, until mixture thickens slightly, about 20 minutes, stirring occasionally.

Spoon chicken mixture into taco shells and sprinkle with cheese. Top each taco with a dollop of sour cream and serve. Makes 8 tacos.

CRISPY BEER BATTER FISH FILETS

1 cup	**flour,** plus extra for dusting
2 tablespoons	**paprika**
2 teaspoons	**garlic powder**
1 1/2 teaspoons	**salt,** plus extra for seasoning
1 teaspoon	**pepper,** plus extra for seasoning
1 can or bottle (12 ounces)	**lager beer**
2	**egg whites**
2 quarts	**vegetable oil,** for frying
8 (4 ounces each)	**cod filets**
1 cup	**tartar sauce**
	lemon wedges

In a medium bowl, whisk together 1 cup flour, paprika, garlic powder, 1 1/2 teaspoons salt, and 1 teaspoon pepper. Add the beer and whisk until smooth.

In a medium bowl, beat the egg whites with an electric mixer at medium speed until stiff. Fold the egg whites into the batter.

Heat oil in a deep fryer or large, heavy bottomed saucepan to 365 degrees. Season cod filets with salt and pepper and dust with flour, shaking off excess. Dip one filet at a time in the batter and drop in the hot oil. Cook filet, turning once, until both sides are golden brown. Drain on paper towels and repeat with remaining filets. Serve warm with tartar sauce and lemon wedges. Makes 8 servings.

EXTRA CRISPY FRIED CHICKEN

4 ¹/₃ cups	**flour,** divided
I tablespoon	**garlic salt**
2 ¹/₄ teaspoons	**pepper,** divided
I tablespoon	**paprika**
¹/₂ teaspoon	**poultry seasoning**
I teaspoon	**seasoned salt**
2	**egg yolks,** beaten
I can or bottle (12 ounces)	**lager beer**
I quart	**vegetable oil,** for frying
I (3 pound)	**whole chicken,** cut into pieces*

In a medium bowl, whisk together 3 cups of flour, garlic salt, 2 teaspoons pepper, paprika, and poultry seasoning.

In a separate bowl, whisk together the remaining 1 ¹/₃ cups flour, seasoned salt, ¹/₄ teaspoon pepper, egg yolks, and beer.

Heat the oil in a deep fryer or large, heavy bottomed saucepan to 350 degrees. Rinse the chicken pieces in water, shake off excess, and dip in the dry flour mixture. Shake off excess and dip in the beer batter; dip in the dry mix once more. Carefully fry chicken pieces in the hot oil, turning several times, until they are deep golden brown and an instant-read thermometer inserted into thickest part of the chicken registers 165 degrees, about 10 minutes for wings and 12 minutes for thighs, legs, and breasts. Drain chicken on paper towels before serving. Makes 6 servings.

*Your butcher or grocer's meat department can cut up a whole chicken, or you can use 3 pounds of your favorite chicken pieces.

BEER CAN CHICKEN

2 teaspoons	**salt**
1 1/2 teaspoons	**onion powder**
1 1/2 teaspoons	**garlic powder**
1/2 teaspoon	**paprika**
1/2 teaspoon	**ground thyme**
1/2 teaspoon	**ground sage**
1/2 teaspoon	**pepper**
1 (4–5 pound)	**whole chicken,** neck, giblets, and excess fat removed
2 tablespoons	**vegetable oil**
1 can (12 ounces)	**beer**

In a small bowl, combine the salt, onion powder, garlic powder, paprika, thyme, sage, and pepper; reserve. Rinse chicken inside and out, and pat dry with paper towels. Rub chicken lightly with oil, and rub the inside and outside with the spice mixture. Set aside.

Prepare the grill for indirect cooking over high heat. Open beer can, drink or discard 1/2 of the contents, and place on a cutting board. Holding a chicken leg in each hand, place the bird cavity over the beer can. Carefully transfer the beer can and chicken to the center of the grill, balancing the 2 chicken legs and can like a tripod over indirect heat. Cover the grill and cook the chicken until cooked through and an instant-read thermometer inserted into the thickest part of the thigh registers 165 degrees, 45–60 minutes. (If using charcoal, you may need to add more to maintain heat.) Remove chicken from grill and beer can and let rest for 10 minutes before carving. Makes 4–6 servings.

SLOW COOKER BEER FRENCH DIP

4 pounds	**rump roast**
I can (10.5 ounces) or 1 1/4 cups	**beef stock or broth**
I can (10.5 ounces)	**condensed French onion soup**
I can or bottle (12 ounces)	**regular or non-alcoholic beer**
8–10	**French rolls**
2 tablespoons	**butter,** softened

Trim excess fat from the rump roast, and place in a 4- to 6-quart slow cooker. Add the beef stock, onion soup, and beer. Cook on low setting for 7 hours.

Preheat oven to 350 degrees. Split the rolls and spread with butter. Place the rolls in the oven and bake until heated through and just starting to brown, about 8–10 minutes. Remove from oven and set aside.

Remove the rump roast from the slow cooker and transfer to a cutting board. Tent with aluminum foil and rest for 10 minutes. Carefully pour the broth mixture into small serving bowls for dipping. Slice the meat on the diagonal, and arrange on the rolls. Cut each sandwich in half and serve with broth. Makes 8–10 servings.

EASY GLAZED CORNED BEEF

4 pounds	**corned beef brisket**
I can or bottle (12 ounces)	**stout beer,** such as Guinness, divided
I teaspoon	**pepper**
I cup	**brown sugar**

Preheat oven to 300 degrees.

Rinse the brisket completely and pat dry. Pour $^1/_4$ cup beer in a small dish. Brush the brisket with the beer and sprinkle it evenly with the pepper. Rub the brown sugar on the brisket to coat, and transfer to a rack in a roasting pan or Dutch oven. Pour the remaining beer in the bottom of the pan.

Cover tightly with lid or aluminum foil and bake for $2^1/_2$ hours. Allow to rest 5 minutes before slicing against the grain. Makes 10–12 servings.

GRILLED BEER BRATWURST

6 cans or bottles (12 ounces each)	**regular or non-alcoholic beer**
3 pounds	**bratwurst sausages**
2	**onions,** thinly sliced
1	**red bell pepper,** seeded and chopped
2 teaspoons	**salt**
1 1/2 teaspoons	**pepper**
10–12	**hoagie rolls**
3 tablespoons	**butter,** softened

Combine the beer, bratwurst, onions, bell pepper, salt, and pepper in a large pot over medium heat. Bring mixture to a boil and reduce heat to medium-low. Simmer, covered, for 30 minutes.

Preheat oven to 350 degrees. Split rolls and spread with butter. Place rolls in the oven and bake until heated through and just starting to brown, about 8–10 minutes. Remove from oven and set aside.

Preheat grill to medium-high and lightly oil grate. Use tongs to remove bratwurst from the pot to a platter. Carefully pour the beer mixture through a mesh strainer, discarding cooking liquid. Return the onion-pepper mixture to the pot, cover, and keep warm. Grill bratwurst, turning often, until evenly browned, about 8–12 minutes. Serve hot on toasted hoagie rolls, topped with the onion-pepper mixture. Makes 10–12 servings.

BEST BEEF BRISKET

1 (3 pound)	**beef brisket,** trimmed of fat
1/2 teaspoon	**salt**
1/2 teaspoon	**pepper**
1	**medium onion,** thinly sliced
1 can or bottle (12 ounces)	**beer**
1 bottle (12 ounces)	**chili sauce**
3/4 cup	**packed dark brown sugar**

Preheat oven to 325 degrees.

Season the brisket on all sides with salt and pepper, and place in a glass baking dish. Spread the sliced onions evenly on top. In a medium bowl, whisk together the beer, chili sauce, and brown sugar. Pour over the roast and cover the dish tightly with aluminum foil. Bake for 3 hours.

Remove the aluminum foil and bake for an additional 30 minutes. Remove from oven and transfer the brisket to a cutting board. Tent with aluminum foil and rest for 10 minutes. Slice brisket thinly against the grain, return to the baking dish, and spoon the pan juices over top before serving. Makes 10 servings.

SPAGHETTI WITH BEER-BRAISED MEATBALLS

I pound	**ground beef**
1/2 cup	**Italian seasoned breadcrumbs**
2	**eggs,** lightly beaten
1/3 cup	**finely chopped onion**
1/2 cup	**grated Parmesan cheese**
2 cloves	**garlic,** peeled and minced
1/4 teaspoon	**salt**
1/2 teaspoon	**pepper**
I can or bottle (12 ounces)	**regular or non-alcoholic beer**
1 1/2 cups	**tomato sauce**
1/2 cup	**ketchup**
2 tablespoons	**tomato paste**
1/4 cup	**packed dark brown sugar**
I pound	**spaghetti noodles,** cooked according to package directions

Preheat oven to 400 degrees. Line a broiler pan with aluminum foil and spray rack with nonstick cooking spray.

In a large bowl, combine the ground beef, breadcrumbs, eggs, onion, Parmesan cheese, garlic, salt, and pepper; mix thoroughly. Shape into 1-inch meatballs and arrange on the broiling rack. Bake for 10–12 minutes, or until lightly browned.

In a large pot, combine the beer, tomato sauce, ketchup, tomato paste, and brown sugar. Cook over medium-high heat until mixture just comes to a boil. Add meatballs and reduce heat to simmering. Cover and simmer for 20 minutes, stirring occasionally. Serve sauce and meatballs over hot, cooked spaghetti noodles. Makes 6–8 servings.

SPICY SWEET
SLOW-COOKED PULLED PORK

1 (3–4 pound)	**boneless pork shoulder butt roast**
1 can (15 ounces)	**tomato sauce**
1 can or bottle (12 ounces)	**beer**
1 cup	**packed dark brown sugar**
$^1/_2$ cup	**honey**
$^1/_4$ cup	**tomato paste**
3 tablespoons	**paprika**
4 teaspoons	**garlic powder**
1 $^1/_2$ teaspoons	**crushed red pepper flakes**
1 teaspoon	**salt**
1 tablespoon	**liquid smoke flavoring**
8–10	**hamburger buns,** split

Place roast in a 4- to 6-quart slow cooker. In a large bowl, combine tomato sauce, beer, brown sugar, honey, tomato paste, paprika, garlic powder, red pepper flakes, salt, and liquid smoke. Whisk thoroughly and pour the mixture over the roast. Cover and cook on low for 6–8 hours, or until meat is tender.

Use tongs to transfer roast to a cutting board. Tent with aluminum foil and rest for 10–15 minutes. When meat is cool enough to handle, chop or shred with forks. Skim fat from cooking juices. Return meat to slow cooker and heat for 10 minutes. Arrange the hamburger bun bottoms on individual serving plates and top each with a generous portion of pulled pork and sauce; add bun tops and serve. Makes 8–10 servings.

CHICKEN AND MUSHROOM RISOTTO

4	**split chicken breasts**
	salt and pepper, to taste
3 tablespoons	**olive oil,** divided
1	**large shallot,** thinly sliced
2 cups	**sliced mushrooms**
4 cloves	**garlic,** minced, divided
3 tablespoons	**butter,** divided
2 cans or bottles (12 ounces each)	**beer,** divided
1 1/2 cups	**Arborio rice**
5 cups	**chicken stock or broth,** warmed
1/4 cup	**grated Parmesan cheese**

Preheat oven to 375 degrees. Season chicken with salt and pepper. Heat 2 tablespoons of oil in a large, oven-safe frying pan over medium-high heat. Cook the chicken skin-side down until golden brown, 2–3 minutes. Turn and cook for another 2 minutes. Add shallot, mushrooms, half of the garlic, and 2 tablespoons butter; cook for 3 minutes. Add 1 can of beer. Cook for 2 minutes. Carefully place frying pan in oven and bake, uncovered for 30 minutes.

Heat 1 tablespoon olive oil and 1 tablespoon butter in a large saucepan over medium heat. Add remaining garlic and cook for 1 minute. Add rice and stir to coat. Cook until opaque, about 3–4 minutes, stirring constantly. Add remaining beer and stir constantly until fully absorbed. Add 1/2 cup broth to the rice, and stir until the broth is absorbed. Continue adding broth 1/2 cup at a time, stirring constantly, until the liquid is absorbed and the rice is al dente, about 30 minutes. Remove from heat, stir in cheese, and season with salt and pepper. Remove the chicken from the oven and cool for 5 minutes. Serve chicken over risotto and top with mushrooms and pan drippings. Makes 4 servings.

HONEY MUSTARD ROAST PORK

1 can or bottle (12 ounces)	**regular or non-alcoholic beer**
$3/4$ cup	**Dijon mustard**
$2/3$ cup	**honey**
$1/2$ cup	**olive oil**
6 cloves	**garlic,** peeled and minced
2 teaspoons	**crushed dried rosemary**
1 (2–$2^1/2$ pound)	**boneless pork loin roast**
$1/2$ cup	**heavy whipping cream**

In a small bowl, whisk together the beer, mustard, honey, oil, garlic, and rosemary. Pour half of the marinade in a covered container and refrigerate. Pour the other half in a large ziplock bag. Add the roast, seal the bag, and turn to coat. Refrigerate for at least 2 hours or overnight.

Preheat oven to 350 degrees. Arrange a rack in a roasting pan. Drain and discard the marinade from the pork, and transfer to roasting pan. Bake for 55–60 minutes, or until an instant-read thermometer inserted into the thickest part of the roast registers 160 degrees. Transfer the roast to a cutting board and tent with aluminum foil. Let stand for 10 minutes.

Pour the pan drippings and the reserved marinade into a small saucepan. Add the cream and whisk to combine. Cook over medium heat until mixture boils. Reduce heat and simmer, uncovered, until slightly reduced and thickened, about 10 minutes. Slice the pork in thin slices and serve with the sauce. Makes 8 servings.

ITALIAN BEEF

2 tablespoons	**vegetable oil**
I (3 pound)	**boneless beef chuck eye roast**
I	**onion,** chopped
I package (I ounce)	**Italian salad dressing mix**
I teaspoon	**Italian seasoning**
2 cloves	**garlic,** peeled and minced
I can or bottle (12 ounces)	**regular or non-alcoholic beer**
2 cups	**beef stock or broth**
10	**deli rolls,** split
5 tablespoons	**butter,** softened

Preheat oven to 300 degrees.

Heat the vegetable oil in an oven-safe Dutch oven over medium-high heat. Brown the roast on all sides, remove from pan and transfer to a plate; set aside. Reduce the heat under Dutch oven to medium, add the onion and cook, stirring occasionally, until just beginning to brown, 8–10 minutes. Add the salad dressing mix and Italian seasoning and cook for I minute. Add the garlic and cook until fragrant, about 30 seconds. Add the beer and cook until reduced by half. Add the stock and bring to a simmer. Place the roast back into the pan with any accumulated juices, cover, and place in the oven. Cook the roast, turning every 30 minutes, until very tender, about 3 hours.

When meat is done, remove from pan and cool slightly. Cut the meat into I-inch pieces and shred. Return meat to drippings and keep warm over medium heat.

Spread rolls with butter and arrange on a baking sheet. Bake until rolls are heated through and just starting to brown, about 10 minutes. Serve the meat on warmed rolls with pan drippings to dip. Makes 10 servings.

BEER-BRAISED POT ROAST

2 tablespoons	**vegetable oil**
1 (3 pound)	**boneless beef chuck roast**
	salt and pepper, to taste
1 can or bottle (12 ounces)	**regular or non-alcoholic beer**
6	**carrots,** peeled and cut in 2-inch pieces
2	**large potatoes,** peeled and cut in 2-inch pieces
1	**onion,** roughly chopped
1	**red bell pepper,** seeded and diced
$1/2$ pound	**mushrooms,** trimmed and halved
$1/2$ teaspoon	**dried thyme**
2	**bay leaves**
2 tablespoons	**butter,** melted
$1/4$ cup	**flour**

Preheat oven to 325 degrees.

Heat the oil in a Dutch oven over medium heat and brown the roast on all sides. Season with salt and pepper. Add the beer, carrots, potatoes, onion, bell pepper, mushrooms, thyme, and bay leaves. Cover and cook in the oven for 3 hours. Remove bay leaves.

In a small bowl, whisk together the butter and flour. Use a slotted spoon to remove the vegetables to a serving dish and keep warm. Transfer the roast to a cutting board and tent with aluminum foil. Add about $1/3$ cup of the cooking liquid to the flour mixture and whisk together. Pour the mixture back in the Dutch oven and cook over medium heat, whisking, until sauce thickens, 5–10 minutes; adjust seasonings if needed. Slice the roast and arrange on the serving dish with the vegetables. Pour the sauce over the roast and vegetables. Makes 10 servings.

BEER AND MOLASSES GLAZED BBQ CHICKEN

I can or bottle (12 ounces)	**stout beer,** such as Guinness
$^1/_4$ cup	**olive oil**
$^1/_4$ cup	**molasses**
$^1/_4$ cup	**orange marmalade**
2 teaspoons	**Dijon mustard**
2 cloves	**garlic,** peeled and minced
I teaspoon	**salt**
$^1/_2$ teaspoon	**pepper**
I (3–4 pound)	**whole chicken,** cut into pieces*

In a medium bowl, whisk together the beer, oil, molasses, marmalade, mustard, garlic, salt, and pepper. Place the chicken pieces in a large, ziplock bag and pour in the marinade. Seal tightly and refrigerate for at least 4 hours or overnight, turning occasionally.

Remove chicken from the bag and pour the marinade into a medium saucepan. Bring to a boil over medium-high heat for 2 minutes. Remove from heat and cool. Pour I cup of the mixture in a small dish for basting; reserve the remainder.

Prepare the grill for indirect cooking over medium heat (350–450 degrees) and lightly oil the grill grate. Cook the chicken pieces skin side up with the lid closed until the juices run clear and the meat is no longer pink at the bone, about 30–40 minutes for wings and 40–50 minutes for breasts, drumsticks, and thighs. Baste with the marinade during the last 10 minutes of grilling time, turning the pieces once. Remove chicken to a serving platter and serve with the reserved marinade. Makes 4–6 servings.

*Your butcher or grocer's meat department can cut up a whole chicken, or you can use 3–4 pounds of your favorite chicken pieces.

SIDE DISHES

BACON, CHEDDAR, AND BEER POTATOES AU GRATIN

1/4 cup	**butter**
1/4 cup	**flour**
1 teaspoon	**garlic powder**
1/4 teaspoon	**cayenne pepper**
1/2 teaspoon	**paprika**
1 teaspoon	**salt**
1/2 teaspoon	**pepper**
1/2 cup	**wheat beer**
1/2 cup	**chicken stock or broth**
3/4 cup	**half-and-half**
1 cup	**milk**
1 teaspoon	**Worcestershire sauce**
8 ounces	**mild cheddar cheese,** grated
3 pounds	**red potatoes,** cut in 1/4-inch slices
1 pound	**bacon,** cooked, drained, and crumbled

Preheat oven to 350 degrees. Prepare a 3-quart casserole dish with nonstick cooking spray. Melt butter in a medium saucepan over medium heat; add flour and whisk until smooth. Cook, whisking constantly, for 2 minutes. Add garlic powder, cayenne pepper, paprika, salt, and pepper, and whisk to combine. Slowly add the beer, chicken stock, half-and-half, milk, and Worcestershire sauce; whisk until smooth. Add cheese and whisk constantly until cheese melts and mixture is smooth. Reduce heat to low and simmer, stirring occasionally, for 5 minutes.

Layer 1/4 of the potatoes in the prepared casserole dish, and top with 1/4 of the cheese sauce; repeat. Sprinkle with half of the bacon, reserving the rest. Repeat potato and cheese sauce layers. Cover and bake until potatoes are tender, 60–80 minutes. Uncover, sprinkle with reserved bacon and bake for 10 more minutes. Remove from oven and cool for 10 minutes before serving. Makes 8–10 servings.

BUTTERED MUSHROOMS WITH THYME

3 tablespoons	**butter**
4 cups	**button mushrooms,** cleaned and trimmed
I cup	**beer**
I tablespoon	**chopped fresh thyme**
I tablespoon	**chopped fresh Italian parsley**
	salt and pepper, to taste

In a large frying pan over medium heat, melt the butter. Add the mushrooms and toss to coat. Add the beer and bring to a simmer. Add the thyme and parsley and cook until the mushrooms are tender and the cooking liquid is reduced by half, about 30 minutes, stirring occasionally. Season with salt and pepper. Makes 6 servings.

GERMAN POTATO SALAD WITH BEER DRESSING

2 pounds	**medium red potatoes**
2 teaspoons	**salt,** divided
3	**thick slices bacon**
I	**small onion,** minced
$^2/_3$ cup	**regular or non-alcoholic beer**
$^1/_2$ cup	**apple cider vinegar**
2 teaspoons	**sugar**
I tablespoon	**stone-ground mustard**
2 tablespoons	**vegetable oil**
$^1/_4$ teaspoon	**pepper,** plus extra
$^1/_4$ cup	**thinly sliced green onions**
$^1/_4$ cup	**minced fresh Italian parsley**

Place the potatoes in a large saucepan and cover with cold water. Bring to a boil over medium-high heat. Add I teaspoon of salt, reduce heat to medium, and cook 20–30 minutes, until potatoes are tender. Drain and cool for 30 minutes.

Cook the bacon in a large frying pan over medium heat until crispy; transfer to a paper towel to drain. Add the onion to the bacon drippings and saute over medium heat until tender, about 3 minutes. Add the beer, vinegar, and sugar; increase the heat to medium-high and bring to a boil. Cook until the liquid is slightly reduced, about 5 minutes. Whisk in the mustard, oil, remaining I teaspoon salt, and pepper.

Peel the cooled potatoes, cut in $^1/_4$-inch slices, and arrange in a large serving bowl. Drizzle with the hot dressing, and gently toss to combine. Let sit at least 30 minutes to allow the potatoes to absorb some of the dressing. Crumble the bacon and add to the potatoes with the green onions and parsley. Stir gently and serve at room temperature. Makes 8 servings.

CREAMY CHEDDAR AND BEER BROCCOLI

2 pounds	**broccoli crowns**
2 tablespoons	**butter**
$1/4$ cup	**flour**
$3/4$ cup	**beer**
$1/2$ cup	**milk**
$1/2$ cup	**grated sharp cheddar cheese**
	salt and pepper, to taste

Cut the broccoli crowns into large florets. Arrange in a steaming basket set in a large saucepan over boiling water. Cover and cook until just tender, about 10 minutes. Remove from heat and reserve.

Melt butter in a medium saucepan over medium-low heat and whisk in flour. Slowly pour in beer and milk, whisking constantly until no lumps remain, about 2–3 minutes. Add cheese a handful at a time, whisking constantly, until all cheese has been incorporated and is completely melted. Cook, whisking constantly, for 3 more minutes. Season with salt and pepper. Drizzle the sauce over the broccoli florets and serve. Makes 6 servings.

BEANS, BACON, AND BEER

1/2 pound	**bacon,** cut in 1/2-inch pieces
1	**small onion,** chopped
4 cloves	**garlic,** peeled and minced
2 cans or bottles (12 ounces each)	**dark beer**
3 1/2 cups	**water**
1 pound	**dried pinto beans,** rinsed and picked through for small stones
1 can (4 ounces)	**diced green chiles**
	salt and pepper, to taste

In a large heavy pot over medium heat, cook the bacon, stirring, for 2 minutes. Add the onion and cook, stirring, until bacon is crispy and onion is just beginning to brown. Add the garlic and cook for 1 minute. Add the beer, water, beans, and green chiles and cook, stirring occasionally, until mixture just starts to boil. Lower heat to medium-low and simmer, uncovered, about 2 1/2 hours, or until beans are tender and liquid is reduced enough to cover beans by 1 inch. Add more beer or water if necessary and stir occasionally. Season with salt and pepper. Serve the beans with some of the liquid in warmed bowls. Makes 8 servings.

GRILLED CORN WITH CHILE LIME BUTTER

6 ears	**fresh corn,** unshucked
3 cans or bottles (12 ounces each)	**regular or non-alcoholic beer**
3 tablespoons	**butter**
1 clove	**garlic,** peeled and minced
1 1/2 tablespoons	**lime juice**
1 teaspoon	**chile powder**
1/4 teaspoon	**grated fresh lime rind**
	salt and pepper

With sharp scissors, trim the silk from the top of each ear of corn and remove any loose outer leaves. Place corn in a large glass dish or large ziplock bag, and add the beer, turning the corn several times. Cover the dish or seal the bag tightly, and refrigerate for 1–2 hours, turning the corn several times.

Heat the grill to medium heat. Remove corn from the dish or bag and discard the soaking liquid. Arrange the corn on the grill and cook, turning several times, until corn is tender, about 8–10 minutes.

In a small saucepan over medium heat, melt the butter and saute the garlic for 2 minutes, stirring frequently. Remove from heat and whisk in the lime juice, chili powder, and grated lime; reserve.

Remove corn from grill to a wire rack and cool. When cool enough to handle, remove the husk and silk and discard. Brush the corn with the butter mixture, and sprinkle with salt and pepper. Makes 6 servings.

GERMAN GREEN BEANS

1/3 pound	**sliced bacon,** diced
1/2 cup	**beer**
4 tablespoons	**butter**
1 pound	**fresh green beans,** trimmed and cut in 2-inch pieces
3 tablespoons	**brown sugar**
3 tablespoons	**white vinegar**
4 teaspoons	**cornstarch**
2 teaspoons	**grated onion**
	salt and pepper, to taste

In a large frying pan over medium heat, cook bacon until crisp. Drain on paper towels and reserve.

In a large saucepan over medium heat, combine the beer and butter and heat until mixture just starts to boil. Add beans and stir. Reduce heat; cover and simmer until beans are crisp-tender, about 5 minutes. Using a slotted spoon, remove the beans from the cooking liquid to a dish and keep warm.

Add the brown sugar, vinegar, cornstarch, and onion to the cooking liquid and whisk to combine. Cook over medium heat until mixture boils. Continue cooking, whisking constantly, until thickened, about 1–2 minutes. Return the beans to the pan and stir to coat with the sauce. Season with salt and pepper. Transfer to a serving dish and top with reserved bacon. Makes 6 servings.

BEER-BRAISED GARLIC PARMESAN ACORN SQUASH

2	**acorn squash,** about 1 1/2 pounds each
1 can or bottle (12 ounces)	**regular or non-alcoholic beer**
1 teaspoon	**salt**
1/2 teaspoon	**pepper**
1/2 teaspoon	**garlic powder**
4 tablespoons	**grated Parmesan cheese**

Preheat oven to 350 degrees.

Cut each squash into quarters and scoop out seeds and stringy pulp. Arrange in a 9 x 13-inch baking dish and pour beer in the bottom of the dish. Sprinkle squash with salt, pepper, and garlic powder. Cover with aluminum foil and bake for 30–45 minutes, or until fork tender.

Increase heat to 450 degrees. Remove aluminum foil and sprinkle squash evenly with Parmesan cheese. Bake for an additional 15–20 minutes, or until the squash is slightly browned. Makes 8 servings.

CHEESY BEER HASH BROWNS

1 tablespoon	**butter**
1 tablespoon	**vegetable oil**
6 cups	**frozen hash browns,** thawed
$1/2$ cup	**diced onion**
1	**medium green or red bell pepper,** seeded and diced
$1/2$ cup	**sour cream**
1	**egg**
$2/3$ cup	**regular or non-alcoholic beer**
$1 1/2$ cups	**grated mild cheddar cheese**
	salt and pepper, to taste
$1/4$ teaspoon	**paprika**
$1/2$ cup	**grated sharp cheddar cheese**

Preheat oven to 350 degrees. Prepare an 8 x 8-inch baking dish with nonstick cooking spray.

In a medium frying pan, heat the butter and vegetable oil on medium heat, stirring, until butter melts. Add hash browns and cook until just starting to brown. Add onion and pepper and continue to cook until hash browns are golden and onion and pepper are tender, about 10–12 minutes. Remove from heat and reserve.

In a medium saucepan, whisk together the sour cream, egg, and beer. Cook over medium low heat, whisking constantly, until thickened. Add mild cheddar cheese $1/4$ cup at a time, stirring after each addition until cheese is fully melted and sauce is smooth. Add salt and pepper. Pour cheese sauce over hash browns and stir to combine. Spread mixture in prepared baking dish, and sprinkle with paprika. Top evenly with sharp cheddar cheese. Bake until hot and bubbly and cheese is melted, about 15 minutes. Makes 6 servings.

BEER REFRIGERATOR PICKLES

2 cans or bottles (12 ounces each)	**beer**
3 cloves	**garlic,** peeled and halved
3	**dried small red chili peppers**
I tablespoon	**black peppercorns,** divided
I tablespoon	**kosher salt,** divided
I tablespoon	**yellow mustard seeds,** divided
I tablespoon	**dill seeds,** divided
2 pounds	**small pickling cucumbers,** scrubbed and quartered lengthwise
	distilled white vinegar

Wash 3 I-pint canning jars in hot, soapy water and rinse. Arrange jars in a water-bath canner or a rack set in a deep pot and cover with boiling water. Cover and boil for 10 minutes. Add lids and rings to the pot and continue boiling for 5 more minutes. Turn off heat and let jars stand in hot water.

Pour the beer in a large saucepan over high heat and cook, stirring occasionally to disperse the foam, until boiling. Reduce heat to medium-low and simmer until volume is reduced by a third, 15–20 minutes. Reduce heat to low and cover. Transfer canning jars, lids and rings to a clean kitchen towel to dry. While still hot, place 2 garlic clove halves, I dried chili pepper, I teaspoon black peppercorns, I teaspoon kosher salt, I teaspoon mustard seeds, and I teaspoon dill seeds in the bottom of each jar. Divide the quartered cucumbers among the jars and pack as tightly as possible, trimming to fit if needed. Fill each jar halfway with hot beer, discarding any extra. Add vinegar to each jar to fill within $^1/4$ inch of top of jar, completely covering cucumbers. Cap tightly and shake thoroughly to blend ingredients. Let the pickles sit at room temperature for 24 hours. Move to refrigerator and chill for 3 days before eating. Store in the refrigerator for up to 2 weeks. Makes 3 pints.

BEER-GLAZED CARROTS

2 tablespoons	**butter**
1 1/2 pounds	**large carrots,** peeled and cut in 1/4-inch slices
1 can or bottle (12 ounces)	**beer**
1/2 teaspoon	**salt**
1/4 teaspoon	**pepper**
1 tablespoon	**light brown sugar**
1 tablespoon	**chopped fresh flat-leaf parsley**

Melt butter in medium saucepan over medium heat. Add carrots and cook for 2 minutes, stirring occasionally. Add beer, salt, and pepper, and cook, stirring occasionally, until mixture just comes to a boil. Reduce heat and simmer, uncovered, until carrots are tender, about 10 minutes. Sprinkle with brown sugar and stir to combine. Cook for 5 more minutes and sprinkle with parsley before serving. Makes 6 servings.

SWEET AND SOUR PALE ALE COLESLAW

3 cups	**shredded green cabbage**
I cup	**shredded red cabbage**
2	**large carrots,** peeled and shredded
2	**green onions,** white and green parts, finely chopped
$^1/_2$ cup	**mayonnaise**
$^1/_4$ cup	**pale ale**
I tablespoon	**sugar**
$^1/_2$ teaspoon	**dry mustard**
$^1/_4$ teaspoon	**celery seed**
$^1/_4$ teaspoon	**paprika**
	salt and pepper, to taste

In a large bowl, toss together the green and red cabbage, carrots, and green onions; reserve.

In a small bowl, whisk together the mayonnaise, ale, sugar, mustard, celery seed, and paprika. Drizzle over the cabbage mixture and toss to coat. Season with salt and pepper. Cover and refrigerate I hour before serving. Makes 8 servings.

DESSERTS

CHOCOLATE STOUT CAKE WITH CREAM CHEESE FROSTING

1 cup	**stout beer,** such as Guinness
1/2 cup	**butter**
2 cups	**sugar**
3/4 cup	**cocoa**
2	**eggs,** beaten
2/3 cup	**sour cream**
3 teaspoons	**vanilla**
2 cups	**flour**
1 1/2 teaspoons	**baking soda**
8 ounces	**cream cheese,** softened
1 1/2 cups	**powdered sugar**
1/2 cup	**heavy whipping cream**

Preheat oven to 350 degrees. Prepare a 9-inch springform pan with nonstick cooking spray and line the bottom with parchment paper.

In a small saucepan, heat beer and butter and stir until butter is melted. Remove from heat and whisk in sugar and cocoa until blended. In a small bowl, combine the eggs, sour cream, and vanilla; whisk into beer mixture. In a medium bowl, whisk together the flour and baking soda and whisk into beer mixture until smooth. Pour batter into prepared pan. Bake for 45–50 minutes, or until a toothpick inserted in the center comes out clean. Cool completely in pan on a wire rack before removing sides of pan and transferring to a cake plate.

To make frosting, put the cream cheese in a medium bowl and beat with an electric mixer on medium until fluffy. Add powdered sugar and cream; beat until smooth. Spread top of cake evenly with frosting. Makes 12 servings.

APPLE CINNAMON BEER BATTER CREPES

3	**eggs,** lightly beaten
1 cup	**milk**
1 cup	**lager beer**
1 $^3/_4$ cups	**flour**
1 pinch	**salt**
2 tablespoons	**vegetable oil**
3 tablespoons	**butter,** melted, divided
2	**crisp apples,** such as Granny Smith, peeled and diced
$^1/_3$ cup	**brown sugar**
$^1/_2$ cup	**vanilla, pumpkin, or regular ale**
$^1/_2$ teaspoon	**cinnamon**
	powdered sugar

In a large bowl, whisk together eggs, milk, and beer. Gradually whisk in flour. Add the salt and oil, and whisk the batter until smooth. Cover and refrigerate for 1 hour.

Heat a medium nonstick frying pan over medium heat. Brush with butter (reserving 1 tablespoon) and pour a scant $^1/_3$ cup batter in the center of the pan; swirl quickly to spread evenly. Cook until edges just begin to color and batter loses its gloss, 30–60 seconds, and flip. Cook for 20 seconds and transfer to a plate; cover with aluminum foil. Repeat with remaining batter.

In a small saucepan, heat the remaining 1 tablespoon melted butter over medium heat and cook the apples for 3 minutes. Add the brown sugar, ale, and cinnamon, and simmer, stirring occasionally, until liquid reduces by about half. Fold crepes in quarters and top with the apple mixture. Sprinkle with powdered sugar. Makes 8 servings.

CHERRY BEERY BUNDT CAKE

3/4 cup	**maraschino cherries,** divided
2 cups	**flour**
2 teaspoons	**baking powder**
1/4 teaspoon	**salt**
4	**eggs,** room temperature
2 cups	**sugar**
2 teaspoons	**vanilla**
1 bottle (12 ounces)	**cherry wheat beer,** divided
2 tablespoons	**butter,** melted
1 cup	**powdered sugar**

Preheat oven to 375 degrees. Prepare a 12-cup Bundt pan with nonstick cooking spray and dust with flour.

Cut 16 cherries in half and arrange cut-side down in rows in the fluted sections of the pan, pressing gently. Chop enough of the remaining cherries to make 1/4 cup. Blot on paper towels and reserve.

In a medium bowl, whisk together flour, baking powder, and salt; reserve. In a large bowl, beat eggs until thick and fluffy, about 3 minutes. Beat in the sugar and vanilla. Add the flour mixture and stir just until combined.

Heat 1 cup beer in a small saucepan over medium heat. As soon as bubbles form, remove from heat and add to batter, stirring to blend. Add butter and stir just until combined. Carefully pour batter into prepared pan, taking care not to dislodge cherries. Sprinkle reserved chopped cherries over the batter. Bake until a tester inserted into the center comes out clean, about 30 minutes. Cool on rack for 10 minutes, and unmold on a platter. Cool to room temperature. In a small bowl, combine the powdered sugar and 2 tablespoons beer until smooth. Drizzle over the cake. Let set for 30 minutes before serving. Makes 10 servings.

SPICY GINGERBREAD CAKE

I cup	**stout beer,** such as Guinness
I cup	**molasses**
I $^1/_2$ teaspoons	**baking soda**
3	**eggs**
$^1/_2$ cup	**sugar**
$^1/_2$ cup	**firmly packed dark brown sugar**
$^3/_4$ cup	**vegetable oil**
2 cups	**flour**
2 tablespoons	**ground ginger**
I $^1/_2$ teaspoons	**baking powder**
$^3/_4$ teaspoon	**cinnamon**
$^1/_4$ teaspoon	**ground cloves**
$^1/_4$ teaspoon	**nutmeg**
I tablespoon	**peeled and grated, fresh ginger root**
	sweetened whipped cream

Preheat oven to 350 degrees. Prepare a 12-cup Bundt pan with nonstick cooking spray and dust with flour.

In a large saucepan over high heat, combine the stout and molasses and bring to a boil, stirring gently. Remove from heat and stir in the baking soda; allow mixture to sit for 10 minutes, or until foam subsides. In a medium bowl, whisk together the eggs, sugar, and brown sugar; whisk in the oil to blend.

In a large bowl, whisk together the flour, ginger, baking powder, cinnamon, cloves, and nutmeg. Combine the stout mixture with the egg mixture, then whisk into the flour mixture. Add the fresh ginger root and stir to combine. Spread the batter into prepared pan and bake for I hour, or until the top springs back when gently pressed and a tester inserted into the center comes out clean. Transfer to a wire rack and cool. Cut in slices and serve topped with a dollop of sweetened whipped cream. Makes 8–10 servings.

CHOCOLATE GLAZED STOUT BROWNIES

10 tablespoons	**butter,** divided
2 ounces	**unsweetened baking chocolate,** chopped
1/2 cup	**unsweetened cocoa powder**
1 1/4 cups	**sugar**
1/4 teaspoon	**salt**
1	**egg,** room temperature
1 teaspoon	**vanilla**
1/2 cup	**stout beer,** such as Guinness
1 cup	**flour**
1/2 cup	**semisweet chocolate chips**
4 ounces	**semisweet chocolate,** chopped

Preheat oven to 350 degrees. Line an 8 x 8-inch pan with aluminum foil and spray with nonstick cooking spray.

In a large saucepan, over medium heat, melt together 8 tablespoons butter and unsweetened chocolate. Remove from heat and whisk in the cocoa, sugar, and salt. Beat in the egg and vanilla until smooth. Beat in the beer. Whisk in the flour just until combined. Stir in the chocolate chips. Spread the batter in prepared pan and bake until a toothpick inserted into the center comes out clean, about 30–35 minutes. Cool in the pan to room temperature.

In a microwave-safe bowl, microwave the semisweet chocolate and remaining 2 tablespoons butter on high in 15 second increments, stirring each time until chocolate has melted. Stir until smooth and spread on top of the brownies. Refrigerate for 1 hour before serving. Makes 16 brownies.

CHOCOLATE STOUT ICE CREAM

4 ounces	**milk chocolate,** finely chopped
4 ounces	**semisweet chocolate,** finely chopped
1 cup	**whole milk**
$^1/_2$ cup	**sugar**
$^1/_8$ teaspoon	**salt**
4	**egg yolks**
1 cup	**heavy cream**
$^3/_4$ cup	**stout beer,** such as Guinness
1 teaspoon	**vanilla**

Put the chopped milk and semisweet chocolate in a large bowl and set a mesh strainer over the top; reserve.

In a medium saucepan, combine the milk, sugar, and salt and bring to a boil over medium heat. In a medium bowl, whisk the egg yolks. Slowly pour $^1/_2$ cup of the milk mixture into the egg yolks, whisking constantly; add the warmed egg yolks back into the saucepan. Stir the mixture constantly over medium heat until it thickens and coats the back of a spoon.

Pour the hot custard through the strainer over the chocolate, and stir until chocolate melts. Whisk in the cream, beer, and vanilla. Let cool to room temperature, cover with plastic wrap, and refrigerate for at least 3 hours, or overnight. Freeze in an ice cream maker according to manufacturer's instructions. Makes 1 quart.

IRISH CHEESECAKE

2 cups	**stout beer,** such as Guinness
1 tablespoon	**packed dark brown sugar**
$1/8$ teaspoon	**salt**
$1 1/2$ cups	**graham cracker crumbs**
6 tablespoons	**butter,** melted
$1 1/3$ cups	**sugar,** divided
24 ounces	**cream cheese,** softened
1 cup	**sour cream,** room temperature
2 teaspoons	**vanilla**
3	**eggs,** room temperature

Preheat oven to 350 degrees. Prepare a 9-inch springform pan with nonstick cooking spray.

In a small saucepan, heat the stout to boiling over medium heat and cook until it reduces to about $1/2$ cup. Remove from heat, add brown sugar and salt; whisk to combine. Reserve.

Mix the graham cracker crumbs, melted butter, and $1/3$ cup sugar in a medium bowl until combined. Press into the bottom and $1/2$ inch up sides of the prepared pan. Bake for 7 minutes. Cool on a wire rack.

In a large bowl, beat the cream cheese and remaining 1 cup sugar with an electric mixer on medium speed until smooth, about 3 minutes. Add the sour cream and vanilla; beat until combined. Add the eggs one at a time, beating after each addition. Pour the filling into the cooled crust. Drop teaspoonfuls of the stout reduction on top of the batter and use a knife to gently swirl into the batter. Bake for 1 hour, or until center is set. Cool to room temperature and refrigerate for at least 4 hours or overnight. Remove springform ring and cut into slices. Makes 10 servings.

VANILLA BEER CAKE

1 package (18.25 ounces)	**yellow cake mix**
1 package (3.5 ounces)	**instant vanilla pudding mix**
1 can or bottle (12 ounces)	**beer,** divided
1/4 cup	**vegetable oil**
4	**eggs**
2 tablespoons	**butter**
1 1/3 cups	**sugar**

Preheat oven to 350 degrees. Prepare a 12-cup Bundt pan with nonstick cooking spray and dust with flour.

Combine cake mix and pudding mix in a large bowl. Add 1 cup of beer and the oil and mix just until combined. Add the eggs and beat with an electric mixer at high speed until mixture is creamy and smooth. Pour into prepared pan and bake until a tester comes out clean, about 55 minutes. Cool in pan for 10 minutes, then turn out onto a wire rack and cool completely.

In a medium saucepan, combine remaining beer, butter, and sugar and heat over medium-high heat until mixture comes to a boil. Cook, stirring constantly, for 5 minutes. Remove from heat and cool for 10 minutes.

Transfer the cake to a serving plate and poke it all over with a skewer. Drizzle the glaze over the top and sides. (You may not need all the glaze.) Allow glaze to set for 30 minutes before serving. Makes 10 servings.

BEER-BATTERED CARAMEL BANANAS

1 1/2 cups	**biscuit mix**
1/4 teaspoon	**cinnamon**
3/4 cup	**wheat beer**
1	**egg**
4	**medium ripe bananas**
	peanut oil, for frying
2 tablespoons	**butter**
1/4 cup	**packed light brown sugar**
1 1/2 tablespoons	**brandy**
1 1/2 tablespoons	**banana liqueur**
	vanilla ice cream

In a large bowl, whisk together the biscuit mix and cinnamon. Add the beer and egg and whisk just until combined.

Pour oil to a depth of 2 inches in a heavy pot and heat over medium heat to 350 degrees. Peel the bananas and cut in half lengthwise and crosswise. Working in batches, dip banana pieces in batter and fry, turning once, until golden brown, about 30 seconds per side. Drain on paper towels.

Melt the butter in a large frying pan over medium heat. Add the brown sugar and stir constantly until mixture is thick and bubbly. Remove from heat and add brandy and banana liqueur. Stir until smooth.

Spoon vanilla ice cream into 8 serving bowls and top each with 2 fried bananas. Drizzle the sauce over top and serve immediately. Makes 8 servings.

SWEETS

STOUT ALMOND BRITTLE

$^1/_2$ cup	**stout beer,** such as Guinness
1 cup	**sugar**
1 tablespoon	**light corn syrup**
pinch	**salt**
$^1/_2$ teaspoon	**vanilla**
1 cup	**toasted slivered almonds**

Line a rimmed baking sheet with aluminum foil and spray lightly with cooking spray.

In a large, saucepan, combine the beer, sugar, and corn syrup. Bring mixture to a boil over high heat. Reduce heat to simmering and cook, stirring occasionally, until a candy thermometer reads 310 degrees.

Remove from heat and immediately stir in the salt, vanilla, and almonds; be careful, as mixture will steam. Quickly pour onto the prepared pan, spreading it thin. Cool to room temperature. Break the brittle in pieces and store wrapped in wax paper in a tightly covered container. Makes 8 servings.

BEER PRETZEL TRUFFLES

1 bottle or can (12 ounces)	**stout beer,** such as Guinness
8 ounces	**semisweet chocolate,** chopped
$^1/_2$ cup	**butter,** softened
1 $^1/_2$ cups	**finely crushed pretzel rods,** divided

Pour $^1/_3$ cup of beer in a medium saucepan over medium-low heat. When bubbles just start to form, add chocolate. Cook without stirring until chocolate melts, then stir to blend. Add the butter 1 tablespoon at a time, stirring after each addition until incorporated. Remove from heat, cover and reserve.

Pour the remaining beer in a small saucepan over medium heat and bring to a simmer. Cook until reduced to about 1 tablespoon of liquid, about 15 minutes. Remove from heat and add to the chocolate mixture. Pour mixture in a medium bowl, add $^3/_4$ cup of the crushed pretzels, and stir until combined. Cover and refrigerate until firm, 3 hours or overnight.

Line a baking sheet with parchment paper. Scoop the chocolate mixture by heaping tablespoons, quickly roll in a ball with your hands, and arrange on prepared baking sheet. Pour remaining $^3/_4$ cup crushed pretzels in a shallow dish. Roll truffles in crushed pretzels just before serving. Makes about 24 truffles.

CHOCOLATE STOUT FUDGE

3 cups	**sugar**
$^1/_2$ cup	**butter**
$^2/_3$ cup	**evaporated milk**
$^2/_3$ cup	**chocolate stout beer**
2 cups	**semisweet chocolate chips**
I jar (7 ounces)	**marshmallow creme**

Prepare a 9 x 13-inch baking dish with nonstick cooking spray.

Mix sugar, butter, milk, and beer in a large, saucepan over medium heat, stirring to dissolve sugar. Bring mixture to a full boil, stirring constantly, and cook until a candy thermometer reads 234 degrees.

Remove from heat and stir in chocolate chips until melted and thoroughly combined. Beat in marshmallow creme. Transfer fudge to the prepared pan and let cool before cutting in squares. Store, tightly covered, in refrigerator. Makes about 84 pieces.

BEER CARAMEL CORN

10 cups	**popped popcorn**
1 cup	**roughly chopped pecan halves**
1 cup (1-inch pieces)	**broken pretzel sticks**
1 bottle (12 ounces)	**brown ale**
3 tablespoons	**butter**
2 cups	**brown sugar**
1 cup	**heavy cream**
$1/4$ teaspoon	**salt**
2 teaspoons	**vanilla**
$1/2$ teaspoon	**baking soda**

Preheat oven to 250 degrees.

Spread the popcorn, pecans, and pretzels on a large rimmed baking sheet and stir to combine; reserve.

In a large saucepan over medium heat, combine the ale and butter and bring to a boil, stirring occasionally. Cook until mixture is reduced by $1/4$. Add the brown sugar, stir to dissolve, and boil without stirring until mixture reaches 248 degrees on a candy thermometer. Slowly add the cream and stir to incorporate. Cook for about 5 minutes until caramel is thick. Remove from heat and add the salt, vanilla, and baking soda. (The mixture will foam up.)

Drizzle evenly over the popcorn mixture, and mix until well coated. Bake for 1 hour, stirring every 15 minutes. Remove pan from oven and spread mixture on parchment paper to cool to room temperature before breaking apart. Store in a tightly covered container. Makes 10 servings.

BEER SEA SALT CARAMELS

1 cup	**butter**
2 cups	**packed dark brown sugar**
1 can or bottle (12 ounces)	**beer**
1 cup	**corn syrup**
1 can (14 ounces)	**sweetened condensed milk**
1 teaspoon	**vanilla**
	sea salt

Line a 9 x 13-inch baking dish with parchment paper; reserve.

In a medium saucepan, melt the butter over medium heat. Add the brown sugar and stir until blended. Slowly add beer, corn syrup, and milk, stirring constantly. Cook mixture, stirring constantly, until it measures 240 degrees on a candy thermometer. Remove from heat and stir in vanilla.

Pour mixture in prepared pan and sprinkle lightly with sea salt. Let caramels set until firm. Remove from pan, peel off parchment paper, and cut in generous 1-inch squares. Wrap squares in parchment or waxed paper and store in an airtight container at room temperature. Makes about 96 caramels.

BEER-GLAZED PEANUTS

4 cups **raw shelled peanuts**
2 cups **sugar**
1 cup **beer**
1 teaspoon **salt,** divided, plus extra for sprinkling

Preheat oven to 300 degrees. Line a baking sheet with parchment paper.

In a large pot, combine the peanuts, sugar, beer, and $1/2$ teaspoon salt. Heat over medium-high heat, stirring constantly, until mixture comes to a boil. Reduce heat to medium and cook, stirring constantly, until syrup reduces by half, about 15–20 minutes. Add the remaining $1/2$ teaspoon salt and stir. Remove from heat.

Spread nuts on the prepared baking sheet with a silicone spatula. Bake for 10 minutes. Remove from oven, stir nuts to separate and bake for another 10 minutes, or until nuts are golden brown. Cool on a wire rack for 10 minutes. Separate nuts and store in an airtight container. Makes about 5 cups.

NOTES

NOTES

NOTES

METRIC CONVERSION CHART

Volume Measurements		Weight Measurements		Temperature Conversion	
U.S.	Metric	U.S.	Metric	Fahrenheit	Celsius
1 teaspoon	5 ml	$1/2$ ounce	15 g	250	120
1 tablespoon	15 ml	1 ounce	30 g	300	150
$1/4$ cup	60 ml	3 ounces	90 g	325	160
$1/3$ cup	75 ml	4 ounces	115 g	350	180
$1/2$ cup	125 ml	8 ounces	225 g	375	190
$2/3$ cup	150 ml	12 ounces	350 g	400	200
$3/4$ cup	175 ml	1 pound	450 g	425	220
1 cup	250 ml	$2 1/4$ pounds	1 kg	450	230

 Check out these "101" favorites
for more tasty recipes:

Apples	**More Ramen**
Bacon	**More Slow Cooker**
BBQ	**Pancake Mix**
Beans	**Peanut Butter**
Blender	**Pickle**
Cake Mix	**Popcorn**
Canned Biscuits	**Potato**
Casserole	**Pudding**
Cheese	**Pumpkin**
Chicken	**Ramen Noodles**
Chocolate	**Rice**
Dutch Oven	**Rotisserie Chicken**
Eggs	**Salad**
Gelatin	**Slow Cooker**
Grits	**Toaster Oven**
Mac & Cheese	**Tortilla**

Each 128 pages, $9.99

Available at bookstores or directly from GIBBS SMITH
1.800.835.4993
www.gibbs-smith.com

ABOUT THE AUTHOR

Eliza Cross is an award-winning writer and the author of several books, including *101 Things To Do With Bacon* and *101 Things To Do With a Pickle*. She develops recipes and styles cuisine for corporate and print media, and blogs about food, gardening, and sustainable living at happysimpleliving.com. She lives with her family in Denver, Colorado.